WE CANNOT DENY IT

Dr. Sharon Mari

WESTBOW
PRESS®
A DIVISION OF THOMAS NELSON
& ZONDERVAN

This book is a work of non-fiction. Unless otherwise noted, the author
and the publisher make no explicit guarantees as to the accuracy of
the information contained in this book and in some cases, names of
people and places have been altered to protect their privacy.

WestBow Press books may be ordered through booksellers or by contacting:

WestBow Press
A Division of Thomas Nelson & Zondervan
1663 Liberty Drive
Bloomington, IN 47403
www.westbowpress.com
844-714-3454

Because of the dynamic nature of the Internet, any web addresses or
links contained in this book may have changed since publication and
may no longer be valid. The views expressed in this work are solely those
of the author and do not necessarily reflect the views of the publisher,
and the publisher hereby disclaims any responsibility for them.

Any people depicted in stock imagery provided by Getty Images are
models, and such images are being used for illustrative purposes only.
Certain stock imagery © Getty Images.

Scripture taken from the New King James Version®. Copyright © 1982
by Thomas Nelson. Used by permission. All rights reserved.

ISBN: 978-1-6642-6948-4 (sc)
ISBN: 978-1-6642-6949-1 (hc)
ISBN: 978-1-6642-6947-7 (e)

Library of Congress Control Number: 2022911288

Print information available on the last page.

WestBow Press rev. date: 07/23/2022

"All your children shall be taught by the Lord, and great shall be the peace of your children."

I thank our Father God for His promise to me and my children

I dedicate this book to my 3 children, my 6 grandchildren and my all my great grandchildren.

Introduction

Why did the Jewish priests deny the authority and power of the miracles Jesus performed on earth? Why did Jesus die for us? Why did He have to take on our sins so we could have a pathway to God?

Generally, Christians are unaware of why the Jewish Pharisees opposed Jesus the Lord or cannot see the reality of their beliefs. What is the reason behind the Pharisees' irrational resistance to the Lord?

Because of Adam and Eve's disobedience, there is a terrible death sentence hanging over the head of every human being.

As you continue to read through the chapters, I want to help you understand what the scriptures say concerning Jesus's death and resurrection. To nullify the death penalty, Jesus died in our place as a substitute. Adam and Eve's act of disobedience was our death sentence, our spiritual and physical connection with God, our Creator.

Why did Jesus come to die for us? Are all humans born in sin? What did His death on a cross accomplish for us? He only lived on earth for thirty-three years, and only three of those years to prove that He is the Messiah foretold by the prophets of the Old Testament.

I was confused; my confusion was in understanding how a *baby could be born in sin*. As a result of the work of the Holy Spirit, I became more familiar with our Father God's plan and purpose for sending His only Son. Because of Christ's victory over death, born-again believers are no longer held captive by Satan's power over their lives. We can receive all the benefits of the promises God has given us concerning this life by the power of the Holy Spirit!

Until I became serious about understanding the Bible, I was unable to explain why Jesus came to die for us. As a born-again believer, you are part of Christ's family and a member of the universal church. Merely putting your name on a church roll does not bring you entrance into God's family. An unbeliever will not understand the terms a believer uses to convince them of Jesus's sovereignty and purpose. It is the work of the Holy Spirit to regenerate the heart to be prepared to receive the truth of Jesus's death and resurrection. Paul writes to the Corinthians (1 Corinthians 2:14) that the natural man does not receive the things of the Spirit, that they are irrational and cannot know them because they are spiritually perceived.

My studies taught me that God had a plan to pursue His people since Adam and Eve disobeyed. I wish to help my children and others understand the whole truth revealed in His testimonies. Especially that He said He would not leave us without the help of another, the Holy Spirit.

As my children were in school, I was at my kitchen table reading Psalm 119. For the next month, I committed myself to read it daily. During that time, I heard the Lord say, "Understand this!" I cannot tell you how His words impacted me to understand. I believe every word He speaks is alive and active and will set you free!

As a result of my studies, I learned about God's providential care and the nature and purpose of Jesus's death on the cross. But what exactly does it mean?

God's providential care is when the Father takes care of you even without you realizing it. He makes all things work together for the good of those who love Him. It is the method by which He makes all events of the physical and moral universe fulfill the purpose of its creation.

Imputation is another word that may be hard to understand. It is a legal term meaning our separation from God or our *state of being* in unrighteousness carried to Christ upon His sacrificial death. It is not stated explicitly in scripture. It is a spiritual reality of truth that several passages affirm that Christ bore our sins and that our sins resulting from the fleshly nature were laid upon Him by God to carry them away or to remove them from us. Jesus's shed blood paid the debt of our unrighteous sinful nature once and for all.

The *purpose* is that sound Bible teaching exposes the enemy. It is light brought against the kingdom of darkness. The following biblical events show that those in authority who should be telling us the truth about God's Word still deny it. The first church was attacked and threatened by death to stop using the name of Jesus as the authority to overthrow Satan's activities in the kingdom of darkness on earth today. As the covenant head and representative of the human race, Adam and Eve disobeyed God. By deliberately disobeying, Adam and Eve died spiritually and physically, and because of their free will choice, we became born with the disobedient fleshly nature. God had given Adam and Eve dominion over all the earth. All humanity then is in Adam and under the power and penalty of sin—namely spiritual and physical death.

- "For the wages of sin is death, but the gift of God is eternal life in Christ Jesus our Lord." Romans 6:23

The *nature* was Adam's spiritual death, resulting in physical death, which became our position in natural birth. That is why Jesus told Nicodemus that he needed to be *born again*. We will understand more of this as we read through this book.

Covenant may be a word that is unfamiliar to you. Covenants are agreements entered into between two or more parties. God has been a covenant maker with man since the beginning. These covenants reveal the relationship between the parties. Satan is aware of this as being God's legal system. The Edenic Covenant in Genesis 1:26–3:24 was made with Adam and Eve before the Fall and was conditional upon both remaining true to God. Following are the conditions:

1. Replenish the earth.
2. Subdue the earth and rule the works of God.
3. Till the ground and be a caretaker of the Garden.
4. Abstain from eating from the Tree of Knowledge.
5. Understand that the punishment for disobedience was spiritual and physical death.

You can see that the covenant breaker was Adam and Eve, who were both deceived by Satan to eat the fruit of the Tree of Knowledge. He tricked them by lying and distorting God's Word by saying they would not die.

As part of the covenant, God gave man the authority to rule His creation through the law. *When Adam disobeyed the covenant agreement,* his spirit died (as God had said), and he and Eve were separated from God and His covering. The earth then legally became Satan's. God expelled them from the Garden to preserve it so that they would not eat from the Tree of Life and pass on the condition of eternal death to their descendants. God announced their punishment, but He also decreed enmity between the woman, the man, and their offspring. Her offspring, Jesus, will crush Satan's head; Satan will crush Jesus's heel by his death on the cross. God's eternal plan is that Satan and his demons will remain enemies until the end of the age until he is ultimately defeated. In other words, He said the redemption plan was already in motion. God was satisfied with this one-time sacrifice that Jesus completed on the cross and became the completion of the law and marked a new covenant for those who would believe in His work on the cross. Before Jesus's death, the Jewish law required regular blood sacrifice offerings on behalf of sins. As our new covenant head, Jesus represented us in His life and death as the *last Adam*. By accepting the demand for our righteousness, God the Father declares us justified (as if we had never sinned), forgives us of all our sins completely, and frees us from the power of our sin nature and the tyranny of Satan, who once held the verdict of death and condemnation over us.

Dear reader, take a moment to read Psalm 12, which is said to be a generational psalm that focuses on the future for our children, grandchildren, and great-grandchildren. It reminds us that evil was being called *good*. Our children are under attack from Satan. And I want to help you with a prayer strategy for action in calling God's angels to protect them. Notice that Satan, the god of this world, is focused on blinding all believers. From the beginning, his strategy aimed at blinding the minds of every generation with lies. Just watch the news to hear all the lies and rhetoric put into our innocent children's minds. In this psalm, the Holy Spirit reveals his deception. The main deceptions to be aware of in our lives are vanity, flattery, and blasphemy. The word *lies* here is interpreted as meaning emptiness by several commentators. Have you ever tried to have a serious conversation with a family member or coworker? In response to a question about their belief in God, most say such topics are too heavy. As a vanity lie, Satan keeps you from ever considering the seriousness of life. What is the purpose of your life?

Another form of deception is flattery, which consists of expressing what you want others to hear and listening to what you want others to say to you. If Satan has blinded you with this, you will not be able to see the light of the Gospel of Jesus Christ. Why haven't I asked myself what the Bible says about my lifestyle choices?

The other form of deception in this psalm is called blasphemy. Its lie is defiance. Those blinded will dig in their heels and say that it is their life, and they can do whatever they want. No rules, and I will find my own way. If you look up this word in the dictionary, you will find a description that says it is an act of insulting or showing contempt for God. We need to be equipped with His Word and instruction to have victory over attacks the enemy presents to kill, steal, and destroy.

I have written many scriptures to make it easier to understand what God says. You need to know what it says, not just where it is. It is God speaking to you, not me.

MOMENT OF REFLECTION

- Your Word is a lamp to my feet and a light to my path. (Psalm 109:105)

Historically, passing our words from one generation to another happened within the family unit by word of mouth. No cell phones, iPads, computers, etc. What Mom and Dad said is the same as what God's Word had to say about it. Scripture instructs children not to forsake their teachings. You must learn that you cannot doubt God's Word making Him a liar and still get the benefits you need from God.

QUESTIONS

Would God be a just person to seek to hide from man His truth and then judge him for not understanding it? What was the purpose of God in giving His truth to His people? What questions do you have?

Let's pray.

> Dear Father, open the eyes of my heart so that I may see and comprehend the love and light of Your Son, Jesus Christ, and the power of His plan for my life. Holy Spirit, come and fill my life! In Jesus's name, amen.

1
Chapter
⤳⚬⤳

WE CANNOT DENY IT

In Acts 4, we begin by reading that the disciples' central theme is Jesus's resurrection from the dead. Peter and John had just healed a disabled man, and the Sanhedrin apprehended them for questioning.

• And it came to pass on the next day that their rulers, elders, and scribes as well as Annas. The high priest, Caiaphas, John, Alexander, and many as the high priest's family, were gathered together at Jerusalem. And when they had set them in the midst, they asked, "By what power or by what name have you done this?" Peter, filled with the Holy Spirit, said to them, "Rulers of the people and elders of Israel, if we this day, are judged for a good deed done to a helpless man, by what means he has been made well, let it be known to you all, and to all the people of Israel, that by the name of Jesus Christ of Nazareth, whom you crucified, whom God raised from the dead, by Him, this man stands here before you whole. This is the stone, which was rejected by you builders, which has become the chief cornerstone. Nor is there salvation in any other, for there is no other name under heaven given among men by which we must be saved." (Acts 4:5–12)

Sanhedrin comes from the Greek word *synedrion,* meaning a sitting together or a council frequently used in the New Testament to indicate the supreme judicial and administrative committee of the Jews, which was first instituted by Moses and was composed of seventy men (http://en.wikipedia.org/wiki/sanhedrin).

The Sanhedrin, known as the chief priests and elders of the people before whom Christ appeared, was tried by this council on the charge of claiming to be the Messiah of a new kingdom.

- Then the chief priests, the scribes, and the elders of the people assembled at the place of the high priest who is called Caiaphas and plotted to take Jesus by trickery and kill Him. Now the chief priests, the elders, and all the council sought false testimony against Jesus to put Him to death. (Matthew 26:3–4, 59)

The apostles Peter and John were also brought before the court for spreading heresy, as also were Stephen on the charge of blasphemy and Paul for violating a temple bylaw.

- And they stirred up the people, the elders, and the scribes; and they came upon him (Stephen), seized him, and brought him to the council. They also set up false witnesses who said, 'This man does not cease to speak blasphemous words against this holy place and the law. For we have heard him say that this Jesus of Nazareth will destroy this place and change the customs which Moses delivered to us. (Acts 6:12–14)

The Sanhedrin is said to have consisted of seventy-one members, the high priest being president. There were three classes: the chief priests or heads of the twenty-four priestly courses, the scribes, and the elders.

- And when they had brought them, they set them before the council. And the high priest asked them, saying, "Did we not strictly command you not to teach in this name? And look, you have filled Jerusalem with your doctrine and intend to bring this Man's blood on us?" (Acts 5:27–28)

They were considered the highest court of judicature, ecclesiastical, and civil supreme in all causes and over all persons. Its decrees were binding, not only on the Jews in Palestine but on all Jews wherever scattered abroad. Its jurisdiction was significantly reduced by Herod and afterward by the Romans.

The Sanhedrin marveled in chapter 4 of Acts; they could not believe in these *unlearned* men. There was indeed something different about Peter especially; after all, hadn't he been the one who *denied* knowing Jesus Christ and his association with Him? Now Peter boldly proclaimed that Jesus Christ of Nazareth was raised from the dead and is the Messiah. They could see that they had knowledge of Jesus and His ways and had been with Him.

The psychological and spiritual strength of the disciples is undoubtedly striking. What transformed Peter? When questioned by a servant girl, the Bible indicates that he became unhinged, and now he is a bold spokesman for the faith that even the entire Sanhedrin could not silence? Would the disciples have given their lives if they had deceitfully introduced a new religion? Clearly, why were they convinced that Jesus rose from the dead, for lies do not make martyrs?

Before giving the Holy Spirit, called Pentecost, Peter would have found his knees buckling before any Sanhedrin collection of Jesus's enemies, but this was a new Peter. He waited for the Holy Spirit's infilling that empowered him with boldness to proclaim the resurrection power of Jesus's name in all authority.

The court decided to withdraw from their questioning and opinions among themselves. The Sanhedrin conversation went like this:

- Saying, what shall we do to these men? For indeed, that a notable miracle has been done by them is evident to all them that dwell in Jerusalem and "we cannot deny it." But so that it <u>spreads no further</u> among the people, let us severely threaten them, that from now on they speak to no man in this name. (Acts 4:16–17)

Satan's deceptive work continues. We see Satan's plan is started here concerning the church and is still hindering the miracle works of Jesus. As I see it, our society today is much like the Sanhedrin of the first-century church. The Sanhedrin rejected the truth that Jesus Christ is the Messiah and was raised from the dead and ascended into heaven to sit at the right hand of our Father God. The disciples first preached to the Jewish nation. As we read in Acts of the Apostles in the Bible, many believed that Jesus was the Messiah and received healing and were changed. We also read that many Jewish authorities denied the resurrection power of God and tried to do everything they could to stop the Gospel of the Messiah, Jesus Christ, from spreading. So how has it changed today? What were the Sanhedrin's fears of this truth? What are unbelievers or skeptics fearful of today? Change, meaning repent and believe. They would have to change their whole way of living. They would be held accountable for their lifestyle. The Sanhedrin sent Jesus to Pilate because of jurisdiction, but Pilate wanted to wash his hands of it as they continued to shift the charges from political to religious grounds. Pilate at first declared Jesus *not guilty*, saying that he had done nothing to deserve death! So being very disturbed by the whole matter, he put the responsibility of crucifying Jesus on the Jewish people! The Jewish people had a lot of half truths about the Messiah. As Pilate heard Jesus speak of truth, he asked, "What is truth?" Afterward, he went out to the mob, declared Jesus innocent, and then had him whipped and crucified. It appears that Pilate had accepted the concept of relative truth. To him, it was the truth that Jesus was innocent, but for the Jews, it was the truth that Jesus was guilty. The only way the Jews could kill Jesus was for Pilate to sentence him to the cross.

The Sanhedrin informed Pilate that if Jesus was set free, they would send a delegation to Tiberius Caesar. They were accusing Pilate of condoning treason in one who would set Himself up as a counterking to Rome's failure in upholding their religious law. They reminded Pilate of Tiberius's threatening letter of five months ago. The letter's contents gave him a choice to support the Sanhedrin in their killing of Jesus. Pilate knew that they would pull his golden membership ring with Tiberius's image from his finger and that he would make his exit via the usual means for disgraced members: exile or compulsory suicide.

The *club existed,* as it does today! Pilate's resistance crumbles. It was Jesus or himself, and he, as well as so many others throughout history, opted for himself! Crucifying Jesus was the Jewish decision. The Jews were allowed to set free one prisoner from the jail during Passover. A murderer named Barnabas was set free by the Jews, and they chanted for Jesus's death. In the face of mounting riot conditions and cries from the public, Pilate gestured toward Jesus and said to the centurion of Jerusalem troops to have Jesus scourged and then nailed to the cross.

There are many interpretations of Jesus's arrest and trial, but they agree on two primary hypotheses.

1. Jesus was some political revolutionary, perhaps a Zealot, and Pilate wanted to crucify a rebel.
2. The New Testament documents have falsely shifted the moral responsibility for Jesus's death from Pilate to the Jewish Sanhedrin.

Some scholars fault the Gospel writers for outright anti-Semitism in reporting the events of Holy Week as they did. Some suggest, however, they were just tampering with the truth for political reasons; unless the reluctant Pilate was forced to do so by Jewish authorities, what else could have converted Romans to believe in someone crucified by their ruler? Scribes and scholars who wrote of the early Jewish traditions about Jesus later gathered in a fifth-century collection called the Toledoth Jeshu, which freely assigns all responsibility for Jesus's conviction to the priests, hardly even mentioning Pontius Pilate. Paul wrote the exact version of what happened at Jerusalem in his epistles, as the Gospel would later do. Unless these and similar facts disprove the hard evidence and not the lies of sensationalism, the New Testament record of the trial and conviction must stand as historical.

Was the demonstration of the crucified Christ's resurrection power of salvation, healing, miracles, signs, and wonders for the Jewish nation only? Why did the Sanhedrin want to stop Peter and John from using the name of Jesus if there was no authority or position in that name? Didn't the disciples say that healing and miracles were only for that period? That period was called the dispensation of grace. It began when Jesus was crucified and raised from the dead and continues until He comes again for His church! Other opinions are that Jesus Christ was not the Messiah but only a prophet of God and that He did not rise from the dead.

The disciples were preaching and healing the sick in continuation of Jesus's ministry, all under the very noses of the priestly establishment. Most of the temple establishment were Sadducees, who denied outrightly any possibility of a resurrection even though Jesus proved at various times that what the prophets foretold in scripture about the Messiah is the truth He gave them. What are most of today's worldly humanist and atheist government officials saying about Jesus's resurrection?

Let's think of the various possibilities. If Jesus lived in our time, we would have guarded His grave differently.

- Scientists would have installed sensory devices both inside and outside the tomb.

- Medical experts would have been scanning computers to record any of Jesus's life signs—or lack of them.
- Theologians and philosophers would have been ready to focus anything visible on a lie of every kind.

Or would any of this have happened? Possibly the hints that Jesus dropped about rising on the third day would have gone just as unheeded today as then. Because scientific and scholarly measurement of that Sunday morning's events did not occur, the spiritual power of resurrection itself did! As a result, the earliest narrative claim, the Easter phenomenon, has been vigorously denied, doubted, disregarded, believed, or enthusiastically proclaimed ever since!

Why write again about Jesus's miracles, salvation, healing, signs, and wonders? Because the same spirit of antichrist that was active during the first church is alive today in our society to a more substantial and greater degree. So we need to speak with the same conviction and demonstration of power available to the first disciples. Many people deny that Jesus Christ existed or deny that He is the Messiah. Some may say that He is the Christ, but they deny His resurrection of healing and deliverance from Satan's oppression. As I have researched in my theological studies, there is much evidence that Jesus Christ appeared after His resurrection. And the healing and miracles He performed were as valid as the evidence that George Washington lived and became our first president! When we are taught history in our schools, we read from texts written by historians who base their proof upon actually documented writings of their existence and works. The same is true about the history and writing of Jesus Christ; the Bible is an authentic work of divine inspiration and facts! Not only is the Bible true, but many other historical records will validate the truth of the Holy Scripture. The Greek word *biblia* means book in English and is an entire collection of sacred texts (http://www.gotquestions/what-does-word-Bible-mean.html).

My topic is not the Bible, so I will not elaborate on its credibility. It is an account of ancient and sacred records of the Jewish nation. The Bible is true in what it contains regarding its writings.

I would say that most people today do not believe what the Bible says because they have not read it for themselves! They base their opinion of what it says on others' views, just as the Jews did in the first church. The majority of the Jewish people believed what the Sanhedrin said about Jesus the Messiah, which they said was a lie. They couldn't deny the various truths that Jesus presented to them of the validity of His Messiahship, yet they were not going to allow those truths to be known.

We need to pray as Peter prayed in Acts to see the fullness of God manifest in our own lives and cities.

- Now, Lord, look on their threats, and grant Your servants that with all boldness they may speak Your Word, by stretching out Your hand to heal, and that all signs and wonders may be done through the name of Your Holy Servant, Jesus. (Acts 4:29–30)

If we believe that Jesus rose from the dead and is seated at the Father's right hand, how can we *deny* the resurrection power and authority of Jesus Christ over the devil's works? Most people deny it because they do not understand the plan and purpose God had in mind when He gave His only Son as a gift to humanity. Receiving that gift opens the spiritual understanding of the truth.

In my childhood, my parents and church leaders did not tell me about the covenant promises of abundant, victorious life on earth and in heaven! They did not present the purpose that Jesus became a man and died to defeat Satan's current authority over all humanity. Man's interruption of the Bible meant that I was supposed to believe that I would go to heaven because I knew Jesus. Of course, this is true, and based on this partial truth, it left me to think that whatever attack of destruction or disease came my way to destroy me or distance me from my Lord and Savior was just the way it happens. Then God said to read Hosea 4:6.

- My people are destroyed for lack of knowledge. Because you have rejected knowledge, I also will reject you from being priest for Me; Because you have forgotten the law of your God, I also will forget your children. (Hosea 4:6)

When God spoke to me about this verse, I did not know it was in the Bible. I was so sure that it was Him. As soon as He had me read His declaration in His Word, I knew the truth! There are many reasons why I didn't receive the proper instruction as a child. I cannot blame my parents or the church who was to teach me. But I know that today, the truth of God's salvation plan is not being taught entirely in many homes and churches.

1. People *deny* the resurrection power of Jesus Christ.
2. They do not know what or why Jesus saved them.
3. They cannot understand the spiritual truth without accepting Jesus as their Savior.

John records that Jesus approached a man afflicted with an infirmity for thirty-eight years and did not know him. He asked him if he wanted to be well. The man answered Him with an excuse that he had no one to help him. Jesus simply told him to rise and walk. Immediately the man was made well. What *changed* his mind? The reality of the Messiah?

The teachers of that day *did not* rejoice that the man received healing; they began to plot and establish grounds for putting Jesus in prison and killing him. They wanted to know why or who told the man that he could carry his bed on the Sabbath! Jesus slipped away from the crowd so there would be no trouble, but later the man found Him, and Jesus told him that He healed him and that he should sin no more; if he sinned again, a worse thing would come on him!

This man's experience demonstrates God's saving power to forgive sin and heal completely and totally. What Jesus says to this man is for all of us that sin causes sickness, disease, and infirmities in our lives and to be delivered, and we need to sin no more! Jesus came to take away the world's sin (the consequence of Adam's choice to disobey God) for all humanity, not just the Jewish nation.

We always have a choice to give in to our fleshly lusts or walk by God's Spirit to fulfill righteousness. We must establish our faith and acknowledge that our sinful nature is the consequence of sickness and disease. That a person can receive healing and walk in wholeness today is why I write this book; we need to go back to the fundamental foundational truths of God's original plan.

MOMENT OF REFLECTION

Does a person have the power to get rid of sin and get out of its control?

The war between the flesh and the spirit is an interesting subject for a Bible study. You can ask your pastor or contact me if you need help.

Man cannot get rid of sin on his own. Man must be changed and made righteous by redemption, and this is the only way to avoid sin. God and righteousness are always present, and so are sin and Satan, but if a believer yields to God instead of the devil and walks in the Spirit, sin will never be experienced again in him. If a believer neglects daily prayer and Bible study, they will be tempted to sin if this neglect continues and is yielded to it repeatedly.

Christ's death fully paid the debt of our sin nature, allowing men and women of all ages to be free once again from the sin nature. Jesus Christ is the only way to be saved, and we are given eternal life through Him. God can help you settle that debt by acknowledging that Jesus paid the price with His shed blood on the cross. This debt has caused many to become a shadow of the new creation they were to become in Christ.

Let's pray.

> Father, I come to You today to ask for Your grace and forgiveness for not believing in Your Son, Jesus Christ, as my Savior. I renounce Satan and all his darkness and lies. I ask You, Jesus, to remove all that darkness and unbelief in my soul, spirit, and body. Cleanse me, and make me Your new creation. I believe that Jesus is Your Son sent to die for me on the cross; I believe He died, went to hell, and rose fully alive on the third day. He is seated now at Your right hand and will come again to rule this earth. In Jesus's name, amen.

Now believe in your heart and confess with your mouth that Jesus is Lord! Tell someone about the decision you made.

Do you believe you had a spiritual debt you could not pay?

Do you believe you are a new creation in Christ and your spirit is now born again?

- Therefore, if anyone is in Christ, he is a new creation; old things have passed away; behold all things have become new. (2 Corinthians 5:17)

2
Chapter

THE APOSTLES
WENT ALL OUT

- For the Son of Man has come to seek and to save that which was lost. (Luke 19:10)

Most people you speak to today would not think that they are lost. They know exactly who they are and where they are going. So when an evangelist comes to their door or neighborhood and asks if they know where they will go upon death, most say or think that people will go to heaven because they are good. In most cases, people do not understand the need for salvation or what it even means.

Satan is a fallen angel responsible for one-third of God's angels rebelling. He is also responsible for the lie of death that caused all humanity to be born under his authority. Isaiah, who is the writer of the book of Isaiah in the Old Testament and referred to be the tremendous messianic prophet and prince of Old Testament prophets, prophesied that salvation is for all nations and humanity. Isaiah 49 speaks of future events when God will deliver the captive Jews and Gentiles taken by the antichrist.

> All flesh shall know that I, the LORD, am your Savior, and your Redeemer, the Mighty One of Jacob. (Isaiah 49:26)

This whole chapter prophecies the work of the Messiah. In verses 5–9, Isaiah speaks of the ministry of the Messiah. He says that the Messiah has come to be a servant of God to restore Israel to God. Jesus will be a light to the Gentiles. As a result, God will authorize Him to make His church a beneficiary of the redemptive work He will perform. His accomplishments will free the prisoners, free men from darkness, and guide humanity. In Romans 1, the apostle Paul wrote that he was not ashamed of the Gospel of Christ. He says it is the power of salvation to the Jew first and then the Greek. Paul continued to preach the Gospel to the Gentiles with all confidence, and no man forbade him to do so! You may say, "I am not a Jew, and I am not a Gentile." *Gentile* means any non-Jewish nation. The Hebrew word *goyim*, usually in plural, means all countries except the Jews (https://www.collinsdictionary.com/dictionary/english/goyim).

Paul tells us that the *Gospel* is of divine origin in the first chapter of Romans and promised to us in the Old Testament prophetic scriptures.

In the book of Romans, Paul writes,

- Concerning His Son Jesus Christ our Lord, who was born of the seed of David according to the flesh and declared to be the Son of God with power according to the Spirit of holiness, by the resurrection from the dead. (Romans 1:3–4)

Paul is sharing his enthusiasm for the glory of the Gospel when he says that it is the power of God to everyone who believes.

It is the *dunamis*, the Greek word for power, meaning that it is inherent power, able to reproduce itself (<u>https://biblehub.com/greek/1411.htm</u>).

The Greek word for delivering, health, save, and rescue in this verse is *soteria*, which is the same Greek word used as an example (<u>https://biblehub.com/greek/4991/htm</u>).

The same Greek word is now about health and the same Greek word for saving.

- By faith, Noah being divinely warned of things not seen, moved with godly fear, prepared an ark to the saving of his household, by which he condemned the world and became heir of the righteousness which is according to faith. (Hebrews 11:7)

Jesus came to bring salvation to all men to restore us to *right standing* with God. By disobeying God's one rule and breaking their covenant, Adam and Eve's *right standing* ended. God expelled them from the Garden (His covering and kingdom on earth). Because of their choice, we are now born in a *wrong standing* before God. Their choice is passed down through the generations from Adam to all people of the earth. *Sinners* have been born with a sinful nature under Satan's rule, the god of this world. Satan stole man's position and authority, and only Jesus can bring us into *a right standing* under God's position and resurrection power to deliver, heal, and be set free!

Listen to the typical Gospel presentation nowadays. You will hear sinners entreated with words like *accept Jesus as your Savior, ask Jesus into your heart, invite Christ into your life*, or *make a decision for Christ*. You may be so accustomed to hearing those phrases that it will surprise you to learn that presentation is only a first response by biblical terminology. They are products of a diluted Gospel. It is not the whole Gospel according to Jesus. The Gospel Jesus proclaimed was a call to discipleship, a call to follow Him in submissive obedience, not just a plea to make a decision or pray a prayer. Jesus's message liberated people from the bondage of their sin while it confronted and condemned hypocrisy. It was an offer of eternal life and forgiveness for repentant sinners, but at the same time, it was a rebuke to outwardly religious people whose lives were devoid of true righteousness. Genuine salvation is not only justification; it must include regeneration, sanctification, and glorification.

- Regeneration: When God transforms a person from a condition of spiritual defeat and death to a new state of holiness and life brought about by God. God plays an essential role in making spiritual change possible. As a result, a person of faith in Jesus Christ is spiritually revived.
- Sanctification: Through God's grace, we become more like Christ by purifying our hearts and minds through repentance, prayer, and spiritual practices. According to the Bible, sanctification is defined as aligning yourself with God's will and cleansing yourself from sin.
- Glorification: As Christians, we will witness the glory of God at the end of this world as He transforms our mortal bodies into our eternal bodies in which we will live forever. Paul writes,

  - Moreover, whom He predestined, these He also called, these He also justified; and whom He justified, these He also glorified. (Romans 8:30)

Salvation is an ongoing process as much as it is a past event. It is the work of God through which He changes us into the image of His Son. There is an inward change spiritually and an outward shift in mind and body; our thinking changes, and our behavior changes. We become a new people. Genuine assurance comes from seeing the Holy Spirit's transforming work in one's life, not from clinging to the memory of some experience.

Jesus did not come to proclaim a message that would be invalid until the Tribulation or the Millennium. He came to seek and save the lost. He came to call sinners to repentance.

- But go and learn what this means, I desire mercy, and not sacrifice: for I did not come to call the righteous, but sinners to repentance. (Matthew 9:13)

He came so that the world through Him would receive salvation.

- For God did not send His Son into the world to condemn the world, but that the world through him might be saved. (John 3:17)

Jesus proclaimed the saving Gospel, not merely a vision for some future age. His Gospel is the only message we preach; any other Gospel is under God's curse.

- I marvel that you are turning away so soon from Him that called you in the grace of Christ, to a different gospel, which is not another, but there are some who trouble you and want to pervert the Gospel of Christ. But even if we, or an angel from heaven, preach any other gospel to you than that what we have preached unto you, let him be accursed. (Galatians 1:6–8)

The moment one is grown enough to recognize one is a sinner and repents and believes the Gospel, a moral and spiritual change occurs.

- But I make known to you, brethren, that the gospel which was preached by me is not according to man. For I neither received it from man, nor was I taught it, but it came through the revelation of Jesus Christ. (Galatians 1:11–12)

The very moment a person decides to sin again, he has a moral fall, incurs the penalty of the broken law again, and comes under the sentence of death again.

- Let no one say when he is tempted, "I am tempted by God;" for God cannot be tempted by evil, nor does He tempt anyone. But each one is tempted when he is drawn away by his own desires and enticed. Then, when desire has conceived, it gives birth to sin, when it is full-grown, brings forth death. (James. 1:13–15)

If a man sins, he must be forgiven and restored or pay the death penalty as in Galatians and the above scriptures.

- Do not be deceived; God is not mocked; for whatever a man sows, that he will also reap. For he who sows to his flesh, will of the flesh reap corruption, but he who sows to the Spirit will of the Spirit reap everlasting life. And let us not grow weary while doing good, for, in due season, we shall reap if we do not lose heart. (Galatians 6:7–9)

Salvation is grace through faith.

- For by grace you have been saved through faith, and that not of yourselves; it is the gift of God. (Ephesians 2:8)

True grace, according to scripture, is

- teaching us that, denying ungodliness and worldly lusts, we should live soberly, righteously, and godly in the present age. (Titus 2:12)

Grace does not grant permission to live in the flesh; it supplies power to live in the Spirit of God. Christ came to set us free. Suppose you are dealing with rejection, hopelessness, fear, abandonment, distrust, jealousy, anger, comparison, relationship issues, or family pain. By working through you, God wishes to heal others and yourself. Internally, there is a war between the spirit and the flesh natures for every person. The carnal nature is the part of us that wants to protect, fight, and remain in our pain. That is the part of us that God wants to change. The Bible tells us to live by the spirit and not by the flesh. A Christian's life becomes more meaningful when he or she studies the Bible. The difference between the Spirit and the fleshly nature must be discerned.

MOMENT OF REFLECTION

1. Do you deny the resurrection power of Jesus Christ?
2. Why did Jesus come to save you? Do you believe this is the only way to heaven and eternal life?
3. Do you understand why an unbeliever cannot comprehend the things of God?

Please read this first: 1 Corinthians 15:21–58.

If we deny the resurrection power and authority of Jesus Christ, the first thing that is lost is the centrality of the death and resurrection of Jesus in the apostolic message. How can some profess to be Christian and deny the central message of Christianity? The resurrection is not a myth or an analogical story. It was a historical event that turned the world upside down. Paul said *this is of first importance*; we have nothing if there is no resurrection!

Let's pray.

> Heavenly Father, we agree in the name of Jesus Christ, Your Son and the name above all names. We are two or more here praying as we invite You into our midst. Thank You for this person who is here praying and agreeing with me. Thank You for forgiving them when they did not acknowledge Your resurrection and sit at God's right hand. I am praying with this person who desires baptism in the Holy Spirit. No weapon of Satan can stand against them because great are You that is in them than he

that is in the world. I pray they open their hands to receive and welcome the fullness of the Holy Spirit and will follow You all their days. In Jesus's name, amen.

3
Chapter
ͽͺͽ

GOD'S ORIGINAL PLAN

King David wrote,

- You have made him to have dominion over the works of Your hands; you have put all things under his feet. (Psalm 8:6)

Psalm 8 and other scripture place man at the head of all God's works: the heavens, including the sun, moon, stars, and the earth, including all living things. It makes him next to God in position and power over all creation. In Genesis 1–3, we read that Adam and Eve's purpose was to rule, live eternally, have children, and have authority over the angels. Still, they were brought very low and made subject to death by the sin of disobedience. By Adam's agreement in taking the fruit and eating from it, he broke the covenant with God and gave Satan the rule of the earth. Now a man in his lessened estate is below the angels. Christ laid down his divinity and positioned Himself lower to take man's place. This gift redeems humanity to that exalted position with Him.

God's original plan for Adam and Eve's existence was that they would live eternally and He would provide for all their needs. They were to rule all the earth, sun, moon, animals, birds, and fish. All things were under their rulership. Their bodies were not subject to an aging process through sickness or disease as we know it. God told them what was required to be fruitful and multiply. To replenish the earth, exercise dominion over the planet, not give it to another, and refrain from eating from the Tree of Knowledge of Good and Evil. When Adam and Eve disobeyed, their Spirit died, which separated them from God, and the penalty, eternal death, took effect immediately. Because of Adam's failure, all humans are born with a rebellious nature, and Satan became the *power and principalities.* Adam gave his dominion of the earth to Satan and his kingdom of darkness.

- For since by man came death, by Man also came the resurrection of the dead. For as in Adam all die, even so in Christ all shall be made alive. (1 Corinthians 15:21–22)

How did the problem of sin start? Have you ever noticed how easy it is to sin? It is not necessary to teach how to sin but to do right. Teaching techniques are required for a child, but we do not need to teach a child to sin. It comes down to this: We are not sinners because we sin; rather, we sin because we are sinners. No matter how moral or religious we are, we still sin.

God provided a plan of salvation to restore humanity to the original state of righteousness through Jesus Christ's death and resurrection! The nature of God is to seek and save sinners. From the opening pages of human history, God endeavored to redeem the fallen couple in the Garden. God says,

- I will seek what was lost and bring back what was driven away, bind up the broken, and strengthen what was sick; but I will destroy the fat and the strong. And feed them in judgment. (Ezekiel 34:16)

The Almighty is Savior throughout the Old Testament as prophecy, so it is appropriate that Christ entered man's world as God in human flesh. He was known first of all as a Savior.

- I, even I, am the Lord, and besides Me, there is no savior. (Isaiah 43:11)

This proclamation means that at any time in a person's life before death, if he decides to call upon the name of the Lord Jesus and repent, he receives salvation! *Whosoever* means that all men and women are equal in God's eyes. When we call upon Jesus, we believe that He will save, deliver, set free, and heal whatever we require. It takes that simple act of faith of an unbeliever to accept the truth of Jesus as Messiah and release the resurrection power of Christ through the Holy Spirit.

- Therefore, as through one man's offense judgment came to all men, resulting in condemnation, even so through one Man's righteous act the free gift came to all men, resulting in justification of life. (Romans 5:18)

Because of Adam's sin of disobedience, a death sentence came upon all of humanity without a promise of resurrection, so by the obedience of Christ sent to take man's place, the penalty was canceled and restored dominion over the earth.

Peter's Greek word for *salvation* in his defense of Jesus's resurrection is soteria. The same Greek word is used in many other scripture references as follows and will bring a much fuller understanding of the fullness of God's plan for salvation!

In *Strong's Concordance,* soteria is translated (https://www.biblestudytools.com/lexicons/greek/kjv/soteria.html) as the following:

- saving, delivering, and preserving from destruction and judgment of Noah's flood
- saved from enemies
- saved from sins
- delivered from slavery
- health preservation of life and physical health

- salvation from physical infirmity
- salvation in general: all kinds of deliverances
- salvation from sins

Thus, salvation cannot be limited to the initial stage of redemption as only forgiveness of sins.

MOMENT OF REFLECTION

From what area of your life do you need God's help? Do you believe that Jesus is our deliverer at this time in your life? What has He delivered you from at this time in your life!

Begin to practice a realization of the presence of God in your life. If you have yielded your life to Him, He is with you! He sees you, and He is interested in every detail of your life. He is your partner now, so do not ignore Him in any life activity.

Do nothing that you would not do if He were bodily present.

Say nothing that you would not like Him to hear.

Go no place where you would doubt that He would go.

If you practice these scriptural truths, your life will be happy and victorious and God will make you prosperous in all things of life as you ask; in faith, nothing is wavering.

- If any of you lacks wisdom, let him ask of God, who gives to all liberally and without reproach, and it will be given to him. But let him ask in faith, with no doubting, for he who doubts is like a wave of the sea driven and tossed by the wind. For let not that man suppose that he will receive anything from the Lord; he is a double-minded man, unstable in all his ways. (James 1:5–9)

Let's pray.

> Dear Father, thank You for saving me and blessing me with the Holy Spirit's help for many things in my life. I need Your wisdom as I read Your Word and continue with the lessons this book presents to me. I ask that You bless my family, workplace, and community. Help me to prosper in all things according to Your will. In Jesus's name, amen.

4
Chapter
ɷ

WHAT DOES THE RESURRECTION OF JESUS REPRESENT?

- And if Christ is not raised, your faith is futile; you are still in your sins! (1 Corinthians 15:17)

It is what the New Testament proclamation is all about! It is a guarantee that Jesus *did accomplish* His mission of deliverance from evil and achieved the supreme project for all humanity in triumphing over the ultimate enemy: death. Jesus arose; so will other human beings. Paul expressed it so well in his first letter to the Thessalonians.

- For if we believe that Jesus died and rose again, even so God will bring with Him those who sleep in Jesus. (1 Thessalonians 4:14)

There were over 514 witnesses who saw Jesus after the resurrection. The resurrection of Jesus is one of the fundamental facts and doctrines of the Gospel.

- And if Christ is not risen, then our preaching is empty, and your faith is also empty. (1 Corinthians 15:14)

The whole of the New Testament revelation rests on this as a historical fact. It is a victory over death and the grave for all His followers. The undoing of the kingdom of darkness, Satan has fallen, and the triumph of truth over error, good over evil, and happiness over misery is forever secured.

The pagan intellectualism of the Corinthians caused them to deny the resurrection of Christ's body. Paul makes this message central in the Gospel of salvation he preached to them. The apostle argues for the importance of the doctrine by facing an alternative to denying it!

He argues that if Christ had not risen from the dead, then His preaching would be useless, their faith would be empty and without power, and they would not become saved. There would be no hope! The Jewish belief in the resurrection of Jesus was essential to the whole salvation message, and it is today. Every unbeliever must know and believe that Jesus Christ rose from the dead on the third day and is seated at the Father's right hand. The book of Acts records the continuation of Jesus's ministry through believers.

- To whom he also presented Himself alive after His suffering by many infallible proofs, being seen by them during forty days and speaking of the things pertaining to the kingdom of God. And being assembled together with them, He commanded them not depart from Jerusalem, but to wait for the Promise of the Father, which, He said, "you have heard of Me; for John truly baptized with water, but ye shall be baptized with the Holy Spirit not many days now." (Acts 1:3–5)

Paul's belief in the resurrection, shared by the early Christians, was absolute and unconditional. The Holy Spirit is now the agent and executive of God on earth to carry on the work that Jesus began both to do and teach. Anything less than Jesus's actual physical, historical triumph over death would have obliterated the cause to which He had staked His life and rendered Christianity, in general, a pathetic lot. A literal resurrection of Jesus's body has been denied by non-Christians and by liberal theology. The opposition stems from this basic argument: a physical resurrection, like the other so-called miracles of the dead, is not possible today, nor was it then.

Further proof of Christ's resurrection is written and documented in *The Complete Works of Josephus.* Josephus was a historian, Jewish priest, Roman citizen, and author; he lived from AD 37 to AD 100. Josephus lived during the time the first-century church was alive. He saw and wrote many firsthand accounts.

Antiquities, 18:63–64, says,

> At this time, there was a wise man called Jesus, and his conduct was good, and he was known to be virtuous. Many people among the Jews and the other nations became his disciples and did not abandon his discipleship. They reported that he appeared to them three days after his crucifixion and was alive. Accordingly, he was perhaps the Messiah, concerning whom the prophets have reported wonders. (Sotheby's (1994), antiquities, 18:63–64 In Antiquities (pp. 63–64 essay)

About AD 146 Just, Mark, Dialog cum Trypho. p. 230 - "You (Jews) knew that Jesus was risen from the dead, and ascended into heaven, as the prophecies did foretell to happen" (https://earlychurch.org.uk/pdf/e-books/williams_a-lukyn/dialogue-with-tryho_williams.XVIL2 pg. 35 pdf).

About AD 400, Hieronymus de. Vir. Illustr. in Josephus -Now, he wrote concerning our Lord after the manner:

> At the same time there was Jesus, a wise man if yet it be lawful to call him a man; he was a doer of wonderful works, a teacher of those who willingly

received the truth. He had many followers, both of the Jews and of the Gentiles. He was believed to be the Christ. And when by the envy of our principal men, Pilate had condemned him to the cross, yet notwithstanding those who had loved him at the first persevered, for he appeared to them alive on the third day, as the oracles of the prophets had foretold many of these and other wonderful things concerning him: and the sect of Christians so named from him, are not extinct at this day. (https://Kentbranden.com/2018/11/23/the-testimonies-of-Josephus-(go+takeit)to-Jesus-2/all)

Historical scholars have believed in the existence and proof of Jesus's resurrection from the dead and His status as God's Son. Yes, many have throughout the ages tried to disprove His resurrection. The proof is true, and they cannot deny it!

Had ancient novelists contrived this story, they could hardly have resisted a scenario in which the risen Christ paid a victorious visit to Pilate, Caiaphas, the Sanhedrin, and the Jerusalem mob, finally compelling them to believe what they previously had rejected. The terror, the awe, the hysterical pleading for forgiveness would have made high drama, and waves of now universal praises would have splashed as far away as Rome and converted the Empire. But Jesus made no such appearances to His enemies after the first Easter, which was entirely in accord with divine policy: God never rewards disbelief; He always rewards faith, according to Christian theology.

His obedience secured our justification for death, so He was raised from the dead.

- Now it was not written for his sake alone that it was imputed to him, but also for us. It shall be imputed to us who believe in Him who raised up Jesus our Lord from the dead, who was delivered up because of our offenses, and was raised because of our justification. (Romans 4:23–25)

The Greek word for justification is *dikaiosis* in this verse, and it means the act of God declaring all men and women free from guilt and acceptable to Him (https://biblehub.com/greek/1247.htm). It is an act done by faith and fulfills the Abrahamic covenant Genesis 12:1–3. His resurrection is proof that He made full atonement for our sins, that His sacrifice was accepted as a satisfaction to divine justice, and that His blood was a ransom for sinners. It is also a pledge and an earnestness of the resurrection of all believers.

- But if the Spirit of Him who raised Jesus from the dead dwells in you, He who raised Christ from the dead will also give life to your mortal bodies through His Spirit who dwells in you. (Romans 8:11)

Paul gives three commands that will bring victory to the Corinthians. He tells them,

- Therefore, my beloved brethren, be steadfast, unmoveable, always abounding in the work of the Lord, knowing that your labor is not in vain in the Lord. (1 Corinthians 15:58)

Stay strong in your faith based on the Gospel, and never give up on the work of the Lord, knowing that it will be rewarded.

Who is allowed to use the name of Jesus, and how?

All believers have the legal and redemptive right to use the name of Jesus in asking and receiving from God.

- Most assuredly, I say to you, he who believes in Me, the works that I do he will do also; and greater works than these he will do, because I go to My Father. And whatever you ask in My name, that I will do, that the Father may be glorified in the Son. If you ask anything in My name, I will do it. (John 14:12–14)

From our study this far, we have learned that the Sanhedrin *forbade* the disciples from using Jesus's name as a source of power and authority on earth to bring divine healing and deliverance from Satan's rule. Jesus is the same today as that day of the disciples. It is foolish doctrine that the power of the name of Jesus was only for the apostolic age of the church. It is clear that Jesus was to be with men.

- Go, therefore and make disciples of all nations, baptizing them in the name of the Father, and of the Son, and of the Holy Spirit, teaching them to observe all things that I have commanded you; and lo, I am with you always, even to the end of the age. (Matthew 28:19–20)

The apostles and others were to *observe all things throughout this age*. Jesus commanded the apostles to be empowered by the Holy Spirit to continue His ministry on earth.

Why does this refer to baptizing? Do I need to be baptized? How?

Yes, there are three important baptisms for all believers in this age. In each of these baptisms, three agents are involved: the minister, the Holy Spirit, and Jesus Christ. Three elements make up the baptized believer's baptism: water, Jesus, and the Holy Spirit. The Holy Spirit baptizes believers into Christ and into His body, the church by His power. Following this, the minister baptizes the believer in water. Then Christ baptizes the same believer in the Holy Spirit, provided they understand, ask for, obey God, and have faith in it. According to the previous order, the three baptisms generally occur in this order. Still, sometimes Spirit baptism precedes water baptism, as in the case of Paul and Cornelius and his house. Water baptism usually occurs before Spirit baptism but always after baptism into Christ and His church. It is the one baptism of Ephesians that all men and women must have to be saved and be members of the body of Christ, the church. The baptism cleanses us from all sin, makes us new creatures in Christ, and qualifies us for both the baptism in water and the Holy Spirit. As an outward sign, water baptism is merely a picture of the inward work that brings us into the body of Christ and the family of God. Baptism into Christ is *essential* to salvation. Baptism into water is *essential* to obedience and a good conscience after being saved and in Christ. Baptism into the Holy Spirit is *essential* to receiving power for service.

Remember the scripture where Jesus said that He would be going away but would not leave them without help. He said to go and wait for the Holy Spirit to empower them for service. He said that He would not leave them comfortless. That's what the baptism of the Holy Spirit for service means. You cannot live on earth today without the help of the Holy Spirit. You must receive all three baptisms. Most people do not understand their need to ask for this help from Jesus, our Savior. Find a church that believes in the baptism of the Holy Spirit for service.

In my role as a chaplain, I would tell women about to return to their community after serving their sentence. Do not be a spiritual streaker. Do not go into your day with *only* the helmet of salvation; put on the whole armor of Christ as it says in Ephesians 6. Would you go into a war battle with only your helmet on? No, of course not. You cannot go into the fight for your eternal life with only the partial knowledge of your power over Satan. Putting on the whole armor of Christ means to be equipped with the Word of God and your full baptisms in the Holy Spirit for power to overcome every plan the enemy has to destroy you again!

Then I would teach them about baptism and the armor of God. I planned baptism into the water on several occasions. Most of the women knew that when released from prison, they were equipped to overcome Satan's attempts to trap them into defeat and possible reentry to prison.

For example, I saw one of the women from the work-release program when I went to breakfast at a local restaurant. She said how happy she was to see me! She came and gave me a big hug and was smiling. She testified that she was ten years clean now! (Five during her incarceration and five since she had been out.) She also boasted that she had full custody of her two daughters now and was working and believing God for her continued help! I told her how proud I was and reminded her to make sure she stayed close to Jesus and make the right choices. God is so true and loving, full of grace and mercy. But we all have to *know* Him and allow His Word to dwell in us. When looking for a church to become a member of, I recall telling the girls to meet with the pastor and ask him, "Who is Jesus Christ to you?" If he cannot tell you who Jesus is (Messiah the Christ, Son of God), run the other way!

We must learn the proper use of the name of Jesus in prayer and daily conflict. Whenever it becomes necessary to delegate to an agent power to sign notes, checks, or other legal documents, it is advisable to grant such powers in a written document and record it. Such documents are called power of attorney.

HOW TO GET THE CHRISTIAN POWER OF AUTHORITY

1. Believe that the Gospel is for you.
2. Repent and be baptized; turn to God and renounce all sin.
3. Obey the truth of the Word, and seek God for this power.
4. Ask to be baptized in the Holy Spirit.
5. Walk and live in the Spirit.
6. Pray in faith, *not* wavering.
7. Have faith in your calling to represent God fully.
8. Learn to use the name of Jesus according to God's Word.
9. Ask God to lead you to the "right" church!

MOMENT OF REFLECTION

All men and women have the legal redemptive right to use the name of Jesus in asking and receiving from God. A good Bible study would be to read Ephesians 6 and study the armor of God.

- Until now you have asked nothing in My name. Ask and you will receive, that your joy may be full. (John 16:24)
- Repent and be baptized every one of you in the name of Jesus Christ for the forgiveness of your sins, and you will receive the gift of the Holy Spirit. (Acts 2:38)

Let's pray.

> Dear Lord Jesus, I have been studying about the Holy Spirit. I want to receive the baptism of the Holy Spirit. I want His help to overcome every attack the devil would have on my family or me. I now realize that I am responsible for asking Your Holy Spirit to empower me to subdue all forms and appearances of sickness, disease, or wrong living. I want to live for You, Jesus. Anoint me with Your Holy Spirit to exercise my faith to benefit your kingdom and help me live a prosperous life. In Jesus's name, I pray. Amen.

Now believe and receive the Holy Spirit to anoint you today.

5
Chapter
∞

WE ARE REDEEMED FROM THE CURSE OF THE LAW

Redeem is one of those words that new believers struggle with about the meaning. *Redeem* means to purchase back or to regain possession of a thing alienated (https://ab1611.com/kjbp/kjv-dictionaryredeem.html).

God's plan of salvation was to provide a ransom. Jesus became the ransom to deliver us from Satan's power and his kingdom of sin, sickness, and depravity to place us under the government of the Son of God's love.

- Giving thanks to the Father, who has qualified us to be partakers of the inheritance of the saints in the light. He has delivered us from the power of darkness and conveyed us into the kingdom of the Son of His love: in whom we have redemption through His blood, even the forgiveness of sins. (Colossian 1:12–14)

Believers delivered from Satan's deception are brought into the presence of God, adopted into the family of God, and have all the same privileges as those born in the family. God wants all His family back!

- And because you are sons, God has sent forth the Spirit of his Son into your hearts, crying out "Abba, Father!" Therefore, you are no longer a slave, but a son; and if a son, then an heir of God through Christ. (Galatians 4:6–7)

What is the curse (https://www.biblestudytools.com/dictionary/curse/)?

It results from the covenant law's requirement of obedience from men who are sinners by nature, breaking one of its commands and being guilty of breaking the whole law. The purpose of the law was not to justify or be a way of salvation. Christ could save us only by showing us our helpless sinfulness while the law demonstrated our helplessness. The law's curse fell upon our Lord as we read this verse.

- For He made Him who knew no sin to be sin for us, that we might become the righteousness of God in Him. (2 Corinthians 5:21)

What does the new covenant mean? What is the purpose of a new covenant between God and man? In what ways is it so much better than God's covenant with Israel of ancient times?

Through Christ, the new covenant allows us to have direct access to God. We are no longer separated from Him. There are still some churches today that have you go through them for that access Jesus died for.

Paul writes to the church that Jesus became our guarantee of a better covenant. Paul writes that Jesus is the mediator and there is forgiveness of sins only through this new covenant.

- How much more shall the blood of Christ, who through the eternal Spirit offered Himself without spot to God, cleanse your conscience from dead works to serve the living God? And for this reason, He is the Mediator of the new covenant, by means of death, for the redemption of the transgressions under the first covenant, that those who are called may receive the promise of the eternal inheritance. (Hebrews 9:14–15)

The new covenant made by God is far greater and better than anything else He has offered to men and women. Through the power and might of His Holy Spirit, God promises that He will personally write His ways onto man's mind through this new agreement.

As we yield ourselves to the work of the Holy Spirit, we are enabled by divine grace not to pay attention to the evil things of this world but to live above it. He took the curse that was ours because of the broken law and bore it in His sinless person, thereby buying and setting us free from the curse and condemnation of the law. The blessing of salvation Abraham enjoyed has come to the Gentiles through Christ. The salvation described concerning the Holy Spirit is called the promise of the Spirit. The reason is that the salvation brought by Christ entails a broader and fuller bestowment of the Spirit that was ever possible in the pre-Pentecost experience.

Paul returned to the Galatian church to remind them of their position in Christ. They had accepted the truth and converted. Now other teachers were coming and teaching them that they still had to observe the things of the law. They were trying to put them under bondage again. He reminds them when he says,

- Christ has redeemed us from the curse of the law, having become a curse for us: (for it is written, "Cursed is everyone who hangs on a tree"), that the blessing of Abraham might come upon the Gentiles in Christ Jesus, that we might receive the promise of the Spirit through faith. (Galatians 3:13–14)

He says they were doing so well; what was hindering them that they should not obey and deny the truth? Paul says that if they allow even a tiny lie to come into their heart, it will cause their whole revelation of truth to be in error. He tells them not to listen to anyone who doesn't teach that Jesus Christ redeemed them from the law's curse. They have victory over their sinful nature through the blood of Jesus and the enduement of power by the Holy Spirit promised to them.

The age of law/grace division, in particular, has wreaked havoc on dispensationalist theology and contributed to confusion about the doctrine of salvation. Of course, there is an essential distinction between law and grace. But it is wrong to conclude that law and grace are mutually exclusive in the program of God in every dispensation. Salvation has always been by grace through faith, not by the works of the law.

- Knowing that a man is not justified by the works of the law but by faith in Jesus Christ, even we have believed in Christ Jesus, that we might be justified by faith in Christ and not by the works of the law; for by the works of the law no flesh shall be justified. (Galatians 2:16)

Just as clearly, New Testament saints have a law to fulfill, not the careless mixing of law and grace.

- Brethren, if a man is overtaken in any trespass, you who are spiritual restore such a one in a spirit of gentleness, considering yourself lest you also be tempted. Bear one another's burdens, and so fulfill the law of Christ. (Galatians 6:1–2)

Instead, it is an essential biblical truth.

- Is the law then against the promises of God? Certainly not! For if there had been a law given which could have given life, truly righteousness would have been by the law. But the Scripture has confined all under sin, that the promise by faith in Jesus Christ might be given to those who believe. But before faith came, we were kept under guard by the law, kept for the faith which should afterward be revealed. Therefore, the law was our tutor to bring us to Christ, that we might be justified by faith. But after that faith has come, we are no longer under a tutor. (Galatians 3:21–25)

If we are no longer under the law, does that mean we can continue to sin in this dispensation of grace? If we read Deuteronomy 28, we would find all the curses all humanity was subject to because of Adam and Eve's disobedience. The chapter begins with twenty-one blessings of obedience. When you read this chapter, you realize the magnitude of curses unbelievers are still under today. Their disobedience has caused them to be cursed. Jesus Christ broke all these curses because of our obedience. When a person recognizes that he is a sinner and repents and acknowledges that Jesus Christ is the Son of God and desires to serve him in obedience, will these curses be lifted from him?

All these curses would come upon Israel if they sinned, then God was obligated to bring them about for disobedience.

His righteousness, justice, and truthfulness require this. Under the law of grace, there is no place a man can fail to obey and be blessed by God, for He has promised cursing of disobedience and blessing for obedience. His fulfillment of this has been demonstrated times without number among angels, demons, and men. The facts of this matter are that all persons need to learn to act accordingly, for there is no excuse for failure in man with the provisions God had made for him to remain in obedience.

- No one can serve two masters, for he will hate the one and love the other, or else he will be loyal to the one and despise the other. You cannot serve God and mammon. (Matthew 6:24)

Paul says,

- Even so we, when we were children, were in bondage under the elements of the world: But when the fullness of the time was come, God sent forth his Son, born of a woman, born under the law, to redeem those who were under the law, that we might receive the adoption of sons. And because you are sons, God has sent forth the Spirit of his Son into your hearts, crying out "Abba Father!" Therefore, you are no longer a slave but a son; and if a son, then an heir of God through Christ. (Galatians 4:3–7)

We have that same promise of the Spirit to us. Paul tells us as well.

- But if you are led by the Spirit, you are not under the law. (Galatians 5:18)

MOMENT OF REFLECTION

Given that we are redeemed from the law's curses, why should we bear the penalty of what Christ has paid for us in our bodies?

The purpose of Christ bearing our sins and sickness in His own body was to take them from us, not to enable us to be sick or sinful. Our position changed from Satan's kingdom to God's kingdom.

- But He was wounded for our transgressions, He was bruised for our iniquities; the chastisement for our peace was upon Him, and by His stripes we are healed. All we like sheep are gone astray; we have turned, everyone, to his own way; and the Lord has laid on Him the iniquity of us all. (Isaiah 53:5–6)

Christ fully met every kind of sin, pain, sickness, failure, and need on the cross. We are complete in Christ. Matthew teaches us to glorify God in our bodies. Just as forgiveness of sin is received by faith in the atonement when one surrenders one's life to God, healing is received by faith the moment one decides to accept it.

- For all the promises of God are Yes, and in Him Amen, to the glory of God through us. (2 Corinthians 1:20)

Let's pray.

Dear Father, I come to You today to ask You to help me to seek You first in my day, to increase my faith by giving me the desire to read Your Word every day, and to trust that what You promise is true. I ask You to help me walk in Your way and not my way. To know that as I seek You first, all Your blessings will come to me. Healing and wholeness are made available to me through Christ our Lord. Thank You for all your love and kindness. In Jesus's name, amen.

6
Chapter
వావ

GOD'S PURPOSE FOR HIS SON

- He who sins is of the devil, for the devil has sinned from the
  beginning. For this purpose the Son of God was manifested,
  that He might destroy the works of the devil. Whoever who
  has been born of God does not sin, for His seed remains in
  him; and he cannot sin, because he has been born of God.
  (1 John 3:8–9)

Jesus came to seek and save the lost, and by doing this, He has set
humanity held captive free from Satan's bondage. Through His
death on the cross and resurrection, He destroyed and canceled all
the devil's power over believers of this age, giving them complete
control. Satan thought he had put Christ through public shame by
crucifying Him. We see through His resurrection power that,

- having disarmed principalities and powers, He made a public
  spectacle of them, triumphing over them in it. (Colossians
  2:15)

Disarmed here means that Satan and his forces were stripped
of their power to condemn and kill our race. Due to nullification
(a legal term that made Satan's rule void), Satan's demonic activities
can no longer hold man in sin and servitude.

Jesus paid the debt for man and conquered death. Peter writes,

- Who Himself bore our sins in His own body on the tree, that we, having died to sins, might live for righteousness-by whose stripes you were healed. For you were like sheep going astray but have now returned to the Shepherd and Overseer of your souls. (1 Peter 2:24–25)

Peter is teaching that part of the redemptive work of Christ is physical healing. He says that He bore our sins in His own body. We could be dead to our sinful nature and alive to righteousness and healing.

In Hebrew, the word *nasa* means to lift; bear; carry away; cast, erase and take away (https://hebrewwordlessons.com/2019/01/20/nasa-lift-carry-and-bear-the-weight).

The idea is that of one person taking the burden of another and placing it on himself, as carrying an infant or as the flood lifted the ark.

- When evening had come, they brought to Him many who were demon-possessed. And He cast out spirits with a word, and healed all who were sick, that it might be fulfilled which was spoken of by Isaiah the prophet saying: "He Himself took our infirmities and bore our sickness." (Matthew 8:16–17)

Our griefs are removed by what Jesus bore on the cross (sin, sickness, and pain) in the same way that sins are delivered or remitted. During Christ's few years of ministry on earth, sin, sickness, and pain were not only removed from those who lived then, but God granted our deliverance to all men of all ages. Likewise, if Jesus bore sickness and bore it only for those few, then sin was also only for those few and the rest of the world is still subject to sin and sickness and has no remedy for either.

- Whom God set forth as a propitiation by His blood, through faith, to demonstrate His righteousness, because in His forbearance God had passed over the sins that were previously committed, to demonstrate at the present time His righteousness, that He might be just, and the justifier of the one who has faith in Jesus. (Romans 3:25–26)

Paul is saying in this scripture that God is declaring His readiness to impart His righteousness by faith to those showing remorsefulness and can now be just in justifying them by His grace. God's righteousness that He is so ready to impart to us is all that is right, meaning His goodness as a loving Father.

- Knowing this, that our old man was crucified with Him, that the body of sin might be done away with, that we should no longer be slaves of sin. For he who has died has been freed from sin. Now, if we died with Christ, we believe that we shall also live with Him. (Romans 6:6–8)

Believers should not serve sin. The term *dead to sin* is used frequently in scripture. It is a common expression among Hebrew, Greeks, and Latins. To die to a thing or a person is to have nothing to do with and to be separated from it or him. To live for something or someone is to be wholly devoted to them and have an intimate connection with the thing or person. Having the old man crucified means that one has no further dealings with him. Being dead to sin does not mean that the person or sin is dead. Both are still in existence and the same as ever, but to each other, they are nonexistent. God cannot declare any man or woman righteous or remit one sin without faith in the reconciliation of God and humankind through Jesus Christ.

Jesus demonstrates His power over Satan as we read in the verses listed below. He now displays it over the things sin introduced into the human race: disease and death.

- At evening, when the sun had set, they brought to Him all who were sick and those who were demon-possessed. And the whole city was gathered together at the door. Then he healed many who were sick with various diseases and cast out many demons; and He did not allow the demons to speak because they knew Him. (Mark 1:32–34)

Demons are evil or unclean spirits and servants of Satan. There is only one devil, but countless demons serve the devil and make his power practically universal. The devil never stops instilling false concepts about God and making them weak, nervous, discouraged, and ruined spiritually, physically, and materially. They conspire to keep men in poverty and failure in life to bring reproach upon God and His Gospel as part of their mission. We have won the battle over them; we must now resist them once and for all.

- Therefore, submit to God. Resist the devil and he will flee from you. (James 4:7)

In Mark 5, we read that the demoniacs are victims whose minds and bodies have been deranged by one or more demons, who at will can speak and act through their victims. Jesus delivered several such victims. As God's power was at work through Jesus's sinless humanity, the supernatural world of evil was challenged, and His earthly ministry was characterized by dominion and power. There has been documentation of demons' existence and personalities throughout history since Adam and Eve fell.

We read in 1 Samuel 28 in the Bible of Saul and the spiritistic medium of Endor in ancient divination. History reveals other practices of magic, ancient necromancy, and modern spiritism. A spiritistic method is talking with the dead and a fraudulent deception to contact the demons representing a deceased person. This practice leads a person to hear unwanted voices and be harassed by those wicked spirits. A demon can derange the mind and body.

- And when they had come to the multitude, a man came to Him, kneeling down to Him and saying, "Lord, have mercy on my son, for he is an epileptic and suffers severely; for he often falls into the fire and often into the water." (Matthew 17:14–15)
- And Jesus rebuked the demon, and it came out of him; and the child was cured from that very hour. (Matthew 17:18)

They have a conspicuous role in the government of the satanic world system in promoting cultism and false doctrine and in opposing God's program and God's people.

- Now the Spirit expressly says that in latter times some will depart from the faith, giving heed to deceiving spirits and doctrines of demons, speaking lies in hypocrisy, having their own conscience seared with a hot iron. (1 Timothy 4:1–2)
- For we do not wrestle against flesh and blood, but against principalities, against powers, against the rulers of the darkness of this age, against spiritual hosts of wickedness in the heavenly places. (Ephesians 6:12)

Prayer is the believers' resource against Satan and demons. One of the most significant errors in the Christian world today is accepting any opposition to answered prayer or any delay in answers to prayer as God's will and responding that it is not His will to grant what you desired. As long as the devil can deceive people into thinking that healing is not for this age of grace, he can hold them in bondage and rob them of the benefits for which Christ died. The devil knows the individual disposition of each person, and he will wage spiritual war against each one according to what he knows and thinks will be the best way to keep that person from getting what he wants from God.

Understanding satanic opposition is crucial. One day, the Lord said to me, "Opposition is evidence of My opportunity!" I had to learn how to overcome the opposition through the Word and prayer. For example, I would read many scriptures about faith and love whenever I felt fear about something and those feeling would leave in light of His truth. Then I told the satanic opposition what God had to say about their deception.

Jesus demonstrated His power over Satan and his demons. Still, what was that power that transformed these timid, passive, dull, lifeless, ineffective men into a courageously mighty herald of the message of Jesus Christ? Jesus foresaw the problem of the messengers being overwhelmed by a powerful statement. So he told the disciples at the Last Supper,

- I will not leave you orphans I will come to you. A little while longer and the world will see Me no more, but you will see Me. Because I live, you will live also. At that day you will know that I am in My Father, and you in Me and I in you. He who has My commandments and keeps them, it is he who loves Me. And he who loves Me will be loved by My Father, and I will love him and manifest Myself to him. (John 14:18–21).

The Spirit's arrival would be at a specific time and place.

Jesus left them but then instructed the disciples not to leave Jerusalem but to wait there for the Holy Spirit.

MOMENT OF REFLECTION

When faith seems weak and victory appears impossible, follow these steps:

1. Accept the opposition is coming from Satan.
2. Verify that the promise of God covers your request.
3. Take care not to live in open or secret sin.

4. Make sure that you do not allow doubts or unbelief concerning the promises.
5. You should sincerely want the benefit you are asking of God.
6. Believe in what you ask of God in faith, without wavering, and that it is yours.
7. Let not even a single thought of the contrary cross your mind.
8. Count the thing you have requested as done.
9. Praise God even before you receive what you have asked of Him.
10. Act as if you have received your request.

- You lust and do not have. You murder and covet and cannot obtain. You fight and war. Yet you do not have because you do not ask. You ask and do not receive because you ask amiss that you may spend it on your pleasures. (James 4:2–3)
- Therefore, I say to you, whatever things you ask when you pray, believe that you receive them, and you will have them. (Mark 11:24)

If God has promised that you can have whatever you ask, if you do not doubt, then do not think it may be God's will to withhold from you what He has promised.

Let's ask God for something in your life that you need to meet your needs according to His will. Do you need peace, emotional well-being, healing in your body, recovery in a relationship, financial help, or a new job?

Pray.

Thank You, Father, for all Your abundant goodness of prosperity You shower upon us. Help my unbelief and help me receive all the blessings You have for me as I learn to walk in Your ways. In Jesus's name, amen.

7
Chapter

THE HOLY SPIRIT: THE THIRD PERSON OF THE TRINITY

While the Holy Spirit lacks a body and a name, He dwells within every true believer and is a constant companion as He walks the path of faith. Throughout all eternity, the Holy Spirit has existed as God. He is also called by the names Spirit, Spirit of God, and Spirit of the Lord in the Old Testament. The Spirit of Christ is sometimes used to refer to Him in the New Testament. Throughout the Bible, we see the Holy Spirit pouring His power into followers of God. One chapter cannot answer all the questions about the Spirit's indwelling, just like Jesus dwelling in us. It isn't easy to accept as true the idea of a personal and direct indwelling of the Spirit in each Christian. When I mention God, the Son, and the Holy Spirit dwelling in us, I am talking about the influence of God in our lives. The following verse uses a word picture of *the temple to illustrate* a beautiful sacred place. We should respect God by caring for and protecting our bodies and mind, just like a beautiful temple.

- Or do you not know that your body is the temple of the Holy Spirit who is in you, whom you have from God, and you are not your own? For you were bought at a price; therefore, glorify God in your body and in your spirit, which are God's. (1 Corinthians 6:19–20)

In other words, does this not simply mean our lives bear His fruit as we live under the influence of His Word?

- But the fruit of the Spirit is love, joy, peace, longsuffering, kindness, goodness, faithfulness, gentleness, self-control. Against such there is no law. (Galatians 5:22–23)

History tells us that Luke is the only writer of scripture to produce both a Gospel and the earliest church history, known as the Acts of the Apostles. Luke is also the sole Gentile author in the library of sixty-four other Semitic books we call the Bible. He was particularly interested in telling how the faithful overcame Jewish restrictions by embracing the Gentile world. He was a close companion of Paul, a trained physician, and an eyewitness to many of his described events.

Luke begins his record with the Holy Spirit's dramatic arrival in Jerusalem ten days after the Ascension. He writes what Jesus had predicted on the Mount of Olives before his Ascension.

- But you shall receive power when the Holy Spirit has come upon you; and you shall be witnesses to Me in Jerusalem, in all Judea and Samaria, and to the end of the earth. (Acts 1:8)

The Holy Spirit, the Third Person of the Trinity, has personality proven that personality attributes ascribed to Him as intelligence and volition.

- But the Helper, the Holy Spirit, whom the Father will send in my Name, He will teach you all things, and bring to your remembrance all things that I said to you. (John 14:26)

He reproves, helps, glorifies, and intercedes. He also executed the offices peculiar only to a person. The very nature of these offices involves personal distinction. God's names are ascribed to the Holy

Spirit and divine attributes. *(You can find the scripture for these attributes in your concordance; study them for yourself.)*

- Omnipresence: everywhere at all times.
- Omnipotence: all power.
- Eternity: never-ending.
- Creation is also ascribed to Him.
- Working of miracles.
- Worship is required and belongs to Him.

Before Pentecost, we read that there were only about 120 Christians in Jerusalem. Their gathering place was a large upper room, otherwise unidentified but probably the same chamber where Jesus had had the Last Supper.

Who were the first 120 Christians? They probably included the disciples, now twelve again with Matthew replacing Judas, who had committed suicide; the Galilean follower of Jesus, including the seventy, referred to in Luke 10:1; Jesus's mother, Mary, and his half brother who had now converted to the faith; Mary, Martha, Lazarus, and the other disciples, John, Mark, and Mark's mother. Small in number, they nevertheless formed the nucleus of the most potent movement ever to develop in history. Their mood was prayerful, waiting for the Holy Spirit, for they could not know the time and place of His arrival.

Suddenly, early that morning, at about 9 a.m., a sound like a mighty, rushing wind began to sweep through that upper room, filling the entire house. What followed was even more astonishing. Tongues, as of fire, appeared to rest on believers' heads yet did not harm them in any way! Whether the flames were actual or only apparent is not clear. Still, a word study of fire in the Old Testament shows that flames regularly denoted theophany (the appearance of God), ranging from Moses's law at Mount Sinai. Fire signified the purifying presence of our deity.

What happened next is what gave them a physical manifestation of the presence of the Holy Spirit. Luke reports that unlettered Galilean fishermen and commoners started speaking fluently in foreign languages they had never learned. The tongues were understood by Jewish and proselyte celebrants of Pentecost from fourteen countries from Mesopotamia to Rome, most of whom had probably prolonged their pilgrimage from Passover to include the second great Jewish festival fifty days later.

In Luke's record, the miracle of Pentecost was not primarily rushing sounds, tongues of flame, or instant linguistic genius. But the arrival of God the Holy Spirit, who could inspire and transform a person in such a way, is only half of the response. The other half is the incredible number of converts, miracles, deliverances, and healings that resulted from the disciples empowered by the Holy Spirit. The book of Acts records that the converts grew from 120 to 3,000 and then to more than 8,000. What a way to develop a church! Even more than that, the number of converts after Peter's preaching was that kind of converts. New believers seem to have come from groups of people just passing through Jerusalem at Pentecost, explaining the Gospel was spreading so fast across the Mediterranean area. When the Passover-Pentecost festivities were over, they returned to their homelands and carried their new faith.

As the movement grew, it was apparent that the apostles did not obey the authorities' order to keep quiet about Jesus or promised they would. So opposition grew more assertive, and Caiaphas ordered them arrested again and thrown into prison. Only to allow the Holy Spirit to work to an even greater degree by sending an angel to get them out of jail. As the Sanhedrin became stronger against them, the apostles grew bolder and only gave them more opportunities to witness the whole community of believers.

- But Peter and the other apostles answered and said, "We must obey God rather than men." (Acts 5:29)

As the power struggles continued, a much-honored Pharisee named Gamaliel stood up and asked to speak to his colleagues.

- And now I say to you, keep away from these men and let them alone; for if this plan or this work is of men, it will come to nothing; but if it is of God, you cannot overthrow it—lest you even be found to fight against God! (Acts 5:38–39)

Thank God for wise men! As we can see through the history and the other books of the New Testament, no one was able to overthrow the plan and power of God through the work of the Holy Spirit!

The devil's hold on lives is destroyed when the anointing comes. When the Holy Spirit opens a person's eyes and ears, the person can undertake the authority given by what Jesus accomplished on the cross on behalf of all humanity. God's desire is for all His children to be whole and strong in their position of authority over Satan.

So many believers and unbelievers know so little of Him, and He is God. Many people ignore Him, never talk to Him, and never ask Him to be a daily, minute-by-minute part of their existence. They prefer pleading and begging and becoming irritated when they see no answers. How wrong this is. The Bible says,

- Draw near to God, and He will draw near to you. Cleanse your hands, you sinners; and purity your hearts, you double-minded. (James 4:8)

It's time to do that. It's time to say, "Here I am, Holy Spirit. Come. Walk with me. Help me receive what the Father has for me. Help me hear what You are saying." You may ask (as I have), "Why doesn't the Holy Spirit, if He's God and knows everything, just help us and give us what we need?" The answer is that He is a gentleman who will never push His way into your life. And as for God, He wants a relationship! And the second you say, "Holy Spirit, help me receive what I'm asking for," He comes and helps you receive through Jesus what you have asked the Father. You see, He wants communion and fellowship with you. He's seeking a moment-by-moment relationship in which you can have the mind of Christ.

- For who has known the mind of the Lord that he may instruct Him? But we have the mind of Christ. (1 Corinthians 2:16)

When Peter, James, and John were with the Lord on the Mount of Transfiguration, the cloud settled on them. What is the cloud? A visible sign and symbol of God's presence with Israel. It is the presence of the Holy Spirit. When you read in the Old Testament of the cloud descending upon the tabernacle, you read God's presence with His people. Also, when Jesus ascended after His resurrection, a cloud received Him. Again, that was the Holy Spirit. Psalm 103 says that He made the clouds His chariot. He often came down in the clouds now. He was going up in one.

Similarly, when Jesus returns, He will be riding on the same cloud. When the Lord spoke, where was the voice? It was in the cloud. The Holy Spirit is the one who brings the voice of God into your heart with clarity.

As you continue to seek God, draw closer to Him, and walk in His presence moment by moment, you will see an increase in the work of the Holy Spirit in your life. The anointing gives you power for service, not for goosebumps! Christians tend to think of the Holy Spirit in the context of the New Testament when His power was throughout the creation account in Genesis.

- The Earth was without form, and void; and darkness was on the face of the deep. And the Spirit of God was hovering over the face of the waters. (Genesis 1:2)

As we study the Bible, we need to remember that the anointing of the Holy Spirit, which is the presence and power of God, is sometimes represented as a dove, but He is not a dove. Sometimes He is pictured as a flame of fire, but He is not fire. Sometimes He's seen as oil, water, or wind, but He is none of these. He is Spirit. Even though He has no physical form, He is still as real as you or me. He is the power of the Godhead. When we consider the power of the Holy Spirit who can calm the seas and the storms, can change a person's will, and make blind eyes see and legs straight in an instant, how can we ever deny or even compare His might to anyone or any demon? God's power is like an atom bomb compared to Satan's firecracker power. God wants us to have that kind of power. With that kind of power comes responsibility and a trusting relationship. If God cannot trust you with that power, He will not make it available to you.

- And when they had set them in the midst, they asked, "By what power or by what name have you done this?" (Acts 4:7)

The Sanhedrin asks Peter and John the same question directed to Jesus after witnessing the miracles done by His hand: by what power, or by what name, have you done this?

What they were asking was by what authority had they been able to bring about this miracle. There was a lot of traffic with demons and familiar spirits then as there is today. Still, the Sanhedrin was hoping to prove the disciples of Jesus guilty of death according to this scripture.

- A man or a woman who is a medium, or who has familiar spirits, shall surely be put to death; they shall stone them with stones. Their blood shall be upon them. (Leviticus 20:27)

We have already seen the boldness of Peter, and that was the power of the Holy Spirit and the authority that Jesus promised him. There is no authority than the Father that surpasses or supersedes the authority given to Jesus. Jesus extends a grant of authority to His followers as He extends His authority to all nations and peoples. It encompasses the extension of His kingdom, the spread of His teachings, and the expansion of His authority. Jesus gave us a commission of His same authority in His name today for every believer.

The Greeks had a word for it. In English, we use *power* to cover many situations. But in the Greek language of the New Testament, there were two words for *power*, each conveying significantly different meanings. One word is *exousia*; it represents the power of authority that a king or president or God Himself might have under his position (https://www.biblehub.com/greek/1849.htm).

The president of the United States could be a ninety-pound weakling. Yet under his exousia over the United States' nuclear arsenal, he can incinerate what he wants. Jesus referred to His mandate of authority when He stated,

- And Jesus came and spoke to them, saying, "All authority has been given to Me in heaven and on earth. Go therefore and make disciples of all the nations, baptizing them in the name of the Father, and of the Son and of the Holy Spirit." (Matthew 28:18–19)

Luke, in his Gospel, tells us that Jesus made the grant of authority exousia even more explicit.

- Behold, I give you the authority to trample on serpents and scorpions, and over all the power of the enemy, and nothing shall by any means hurt you. (Luke 10:19)

The serpents and scorpions referred to in this scripture are the devil and his agents. The devil will not be your problem in life if you are a child of God. Because you are born of God, you are superior to the devil and all his kingdom of darkness. Why does Jesus refer to devils as *serpents* and *scorpions?* If serpents and scorpions are used as metaphors for demons, they must have the same features and characteristics as demons.

Here are some characteristics to be aware of:

1. Poisonous: Both creatures are deadly. They use a poisonous liquid that kills. Poison symbolizes the deposit of evil in the spirit world. A demon is poisonous and has the power to inject evil spiritual poison into the life of its victim.

2. Subtle: Snakes and scorpions have a cunning and subtle nature. Unless you become spiritually sensitive, you will not see them coming. Satan, like the creatures, is a seducer and a deceiver, and so are his demons. The devil deceived Adam and Eve and took authority over the earth and humankind. In Jesus's mission to regain authority for humankind, Satan tried to trick Him but failed. Jesus's only defense was spiritually sensitive and alert.

3. Violent and offensive: Yet again, they are offensive and violent. They strike quickly and without warning. It's all about killing, stealing, and destroying you. You must go on the offensive and use the Word against the devil. We crush every demon in the same way we crush scorpions and serpents. The devil and his demons are no longer a factor in your life as a Christian.

4. They can be crushed: Every demon is crushable, like scorpions and serpents. It is no longer a factor that the devil is involved because you have been given authority over him and his demons.

Two things are clear; we have authority over Satan and whatever comes from him, and the restoration of the authority over the serpent, which Adam lost in the Garden. Jesus gave a further extension of His authority exousia power when He told the disciples to pray in His name.

- And whatever you ask in My name, that I will do, that the Father may be glorified in the Son. If you ask anything in my name, I will do it. (John 14:13–14)

When we think of the natural as having power and authority, usually along with that position come keys that allow the ability or access to the thing that we are given that power and authority. Let's say, for instance, that I am the chief engineer of operations for a multimillion-dollar company. I have the keys to all the doors of the offices and operations of that company; I designate the other positions of authority. That's the way it is in the kingdom of God. Jesus, who we have already established is the Messiah, the Son of God, has taken back the position of authority over Satan's power over all believers on the earth. Jesus is Lord over all the world!

The second New Testament Greek word for power is *dunamis*, which carries the concept of resident or inherent strength and force (https://biblehub.com/greek/1411.htm).

Like dynamite! The word is used in Acts 1:8 when Jesus instructed His disciples to wait for the dunamis power they would receive from the Holy Spirit. Temporarily, Jesus is not available on the earth (He is at the head office) in the position of rulership that He has already established on earth on our behalf. God told us through Peter that we (all believers) have designated authority and power over all the powers and principalities of the air, meaning Satan and his demon princes. Jesus said to Peter,

- He said to them, "But who do you say I am?" Simon Peter answered and said, "You are the Christ, the Son of the living God." Jesus answered and said to him, "Blessed are you, Simon Bar-jona, for flesh and blood has not revealed this to you, but My Father who is in heaven. And I also say to you that you are Peter, and on this rock, I will build my church, and the gates of Hades shall not prevail against it. And I will give you the keys of the kingdom of heaven:

and whatever you bind on earth will be bound in heaven, and whatever you loose on earth will be loosed in heaven." (Matthew 16:15–19)

Keys are a symbol of authority in the Bible as well.

In the days of King David, he transferred keys to the person who had possession of property of trust as an emblem of authority and power. So when Peter acknowledged that he understood who Jesus was and was revealed to him divinely by our Father in heaven. Jesus knew that it was Peter to whom he would pass on his authority on the earth until he would return to rule again. Building the church was the first responsibility of Peter as the first pastor and builder. As the keeper of the keys, he would have the same authority that Jesus had from the Father to open and close authority areas. The keys are an emblem of power and authority to do the works of Christ. Whatever he bound or loosed is the fundamental idea.

Key or keys are frequently mentioned in scripture. It is called, in Hebrew, *maphteah*, meaning the opener, and in the Greek New Testament *kleis*, from its use in shutting (htts://biblestudytools.com/dictionary/key).

Figures of ancient Egyptian keys are found on monuments, Assyrian locks, and wood keys of considerable size. The word is figurative of power, authority, or office. The key to knowledge in the book of Luke is the means of attaining knowledge regarding the kingdom of God. The *power of the keys* is a phrase used to denote the extent of ecclesiastical authority.

Again, or once more, Jesus reminds the disciples of their power and position. The legal transference of authority. It is just like a legal paper on earth that gives one person the *power of attorney* over all the property and possessions of another. To ask in faith on behalf of the person giving the authority to handle their possessions properly.

The legal terms *bind* and *loose* are essential for the believer to understand, for they are given in the context of a legal agreement and can only be honored in light of that agreement. The authority and power are delegated to us from Jesus, so we need to understand that we have this power in His name. The Sanhedrin always asked Jesus and the disciples to tell them by what power or authority they had to do this. Thus, trying to get them to refer to another kingdom and charge them with sedition. As we read at the beginning of this book, Peter said very boldly,

- Let it be known to you all, and to all the people of Israel, that by the name of Jesus Christ of Nazareth, whom you crucified, whom God raised from the dead, by Him this man stands here before you whole. (Acts 4:10)

Therefore, we are not subject to the powers and principalities of the air or earth. What Jesus has accomplished for us gives us that authority!

In Luke 10, we read that Jesus had selected seventy followers and sent them out two by two with instruction. They returned to Him with joy and said,

- Then the seventy returned with joy, saying "Lord, even the demons are subject to us in Your Name!" (Luke 10:17)

That is what Jesus wanted to hear then as well as today! We need to understand that Satan still has rule over the earth and unbelievers.

As we read in Revelation, the rest of Satan's destiny and the final victory are doomed to the lake of fire forever. And all the saints are then standing before the great white throne where God opens the book of life. In verse 15, we read,

- And anyone not found written in the book of life was cast into the lake of fire. (Revelation 20:15)

The average person does not understand the real issues between God and Satan. Satan takes advantage of this ignorance and unbelief to hinder the church's effectiveness. Millions of Christians are losing to him. In other words, he is making them think that it is not God's will that they get whatever they need or want in this life. They become fearful of using the name of Jesus in prayer and the daily battle between him and his demons. While the church lives in this ignorance, it will fail to do the works of God that are meant to be evident today in every local church, as they were during the early churches. Any believer can use Jesus's name. No extraordinary faith is necessary to use His name. Just simple, ordinary, childlike faith in God and the work of Christ is all that is necessary to get answers to your prayers. If you read the scriptures I have given you here, you will believe that you will receive. You will get the answers you have been seeking from God.

I want to remind you of what I said at the beginning of this book. The Holy Spirit put the scripture Hosea 4:6 in my mind to read. According to this scripture, I believed that my parents failed to teach us about God's way of life, so the foundation of my family was shattered. We lack knowledge about who He (God) is and what He wants to give us as we follow Him.

- Until now you have asked nothing in My name. Ask, and you will receive, that your joy may be full. (John 16:24)

Jesus conferred this power upon others during His earthly ministry. How much greater is His ability to do so now that He has destroyed Satan's principalities and powers and completed redemption! As Christians, we are instructed to call upon the name of Jesus in everything we do. As parents, we teach our children about God and His ways.

MOMENT OF REFLECTION

Here are a couple of questions to think about:

1. What is meant by "the Christian's power of attorney"?
2. Can you give biblical proof of the Christian's power of attorney?
3. What does it mean to pray in the name of Jesus?

- "Therefore, submit to God. Resist the devil, and he will flee from you." (James 4:7)

We must understand that we are representatives of God and that we are taking the place of Christ in this world to cast out demons. Let's pray.

Dear Father, I realize that I need Your presence in every part of my life. I am adrift on a sea of indecision without You, going nowhere. I choose today to come near You to share my heart, wishes, sorrows, and pain with You. It gives me great joy to hear You say, "You are forgiven, my child." I humbly ask You to draw me and help me seek You and Your way. I want to read Your Word daily; give me an understanding of Your Word. I pray that I will discover what I have been searching for all along: a Father who adores me, a Savior who gave himself for me, and a Spirit who will never leave me. In Jesus's name, amen.

8
Chapter
∾∾∾

THE PURPOSE OF THE GIFTS OF THE HOLY SPIRIT

When we see God's plan from the time of creation through the Fall of man, from the old covenant of the law through the cross, it is easier to understand God's attitude toward all sickness and disease. After Adam sinned, humanity was in a fallen state of being that brought all sickness and the curse of every infirmity that resulted from the Fall. We all have been separated apart from God's original plan.

God could only provide physical deliverance for the children of Israel. We read where He provided healing, their needs, and deliverance from their enemies. Still, He could not do anything about their spiritual condition when God promised that He would raise a prophet from among His people. He was prophesying that His only begotten Son would redeem humanity to God's original plan!

Those who obey God and His redemption plan in all ages are given gifts of the Holy Spirit. We read in Isaiah 63 concerning Moses and how God gave him gifts by the Holy Spirit of performing miracles and leading and teaching the people beyond all the opposition that confronted him.

Every time Moses obeyed, God stretched forth His hand, and He did signs and wonders to deliver His people. From beginning to the end, the law is unchangeable. It is only obedience that gives access to the Tree of Life and the favor of God.

What God did for the children of Israel, He promised He would do for us! *Jesus came to save us spiritually and physically.* The Gospel is the power of God unto salvation, meaning wholeness in spirit, soul, and body. God compels us to command His will be done on the earth.

- Your kingdom come. Your will be done on earth, as it is in heaven. (Matthew 6:10)

Jesus did not work miracles solely under His Deity but in the person of His sinless humanity united to Deity by the Holy Spirit. He gave up His Deity when He became a human. The Holy Spirit worked in the fullness of anointing through the vessel of Jesus's undefiled human nature, which brought about these mighty signs by His spoken Word, occasionally combined with physical agents, such as clay or saliva.

The Holy Spirit's work through miracles, signs, and wonders was to authenticate His Deity and Messiahship. They were also expressions of His love and compassion for all humanity.

With all the miracles Jesus did, they chose to reject the proof of Christ's Deity and decided to kill him, so they have no excuse for their sin of willfully hating God the Father and Jesus His Son.

- And through the hands of the Apostles were many signs and wonders done among the people. And they were all with one accord in Solomon's porch. (Acts 5:12)

The apostles' central theme was still the resurrection of Jesus that makes all the Gospel effective, and anyone who does not believe in it cannot be saved from Satan's snare and receive eternal life. Those who believe are partakers of the divine nature. They have access to God and the freedom to exercise the divine powers that belong to the family of God.

- Grace and peace be multiplied to you in the knowledge of God and of Jesus our Lord, as His divine power has given to us all things that pertain to life and godliness, through the knowledge of Him, who called us by glory and virtue, by which have been given to us exceedingly great and precious promises, that through these you may be partakers of the divine nature, having escaped the corruption that is in the world through lust. (2 Peter 1:2–4)

Scripture records that all the gifts of the Holy Spirit were active in the lives of the believers in the early church after they received the Holy Spirit.

The miracles and healing power of the apostles have appeared to become equal to that of Christ, fulfilling what Jesus said.

- Most assuredly, I say to you, he who believes in Me, the works that I do he will do also; and greater works than these he will do; because I go unto My Father. (John 14:12)

It was a known fact that Christians knew the facts of the Gospel, and God Himself confirmed the truth through His signs. His obedient apostles and prophets performed many wonders and mighty deeds under Jesus's guidance. The main purpose of each of them was to confirm God's Word, prove the men's identity, and demonstrate their words were indeed inspired by God.

Paul had all the gifts of the Spirit.

- But I know that when I come to you, I shall come in the fullness of the blessing of the gospel of Christ. (Romans 15:29)

He believed and received! Many scriptures show the gifts the Holy Spirit gave him. Believers share the divine nature. As members of God's family, we have access to God and can exercise the same divine powers He gave them. Paul taught of spiritual gifts by saying,

- Now concerning spiritual gift, brethren, I do not want you to be ignorant. (1 Corinthians 12:1)

And he ended his teaching by saying,

- But if anyone is ignorant, let him be ignorant. (1 Corinthians 14:38)

According to general principles, the more complex and detailed the truth, the more likely people will be unaware of it. Since the Corinthians were hopeless idolators, they were familiar with supernatural power and its operation. The Gentiles and the Jews practiced magic and sorcery, yielding themselves to demons and Satan. Many Gentile converts were unaware of the difference between these demon powers and the true spiritual gifts and how they work. Paul gave them a law of discernment between good and evil spirits.

- You know that you were Gentiles, carried away to these dumb idols, however you were led. Therefore, I make known to you that no one speaking by the Spirit of God calls Jesus accursed; and no one can say that Jesus is Lord except by the Holy Spirit. (1 Corinthians. 12:2–3)

In other words, any person with power doing miracles and otherwise manifesting itself, if that person calls Jesus accursed or claims that He did not come in the flesh, it is of the devil and not God. Every believer needs the gifts of the Holy Spirit to cope with satanic powers and defeat the devil's works in their own lives and the lives of their family.

MOMENT OF REFLECTION

How can gifts of the Holy Spirit be received?

The disciples received the Holy Spirit and various gifts by tarrying for the enduement of power from on high. The Gentiles received the Holy Spirit baptism while listening to the Word of God. Others received the baptism by laying on of hands. If you do not have anyone with the power to pray for you, you can still get the gift by personal prayer and fasting or the ordinary seeking of God by faith, and He will give you the gifts you desire for His glory.

Let's pray.

> Dear Father, I recognize my need for Your power to live this new life. Please fill me with Your Holy Spirit. By faith, I receive it right now! Thank You for baptizing me. Holy Spirit, You are welcome in my life. In Jesus's name, amen.

It doesn't matter whether you felt anything or not when you prayed to receive the Lord and His Spirit. If you believe in your heart that you received, God's Word promises you did. I suggest that you study the Bible about the gifts of the Holy Spirit. You can find the scripture references in the index of your Bible.

- Therefore, I say to you, whatever things you ask when you pray, believe that you receive them, and you will have them. (Mark 11:24)

9
Chapter
❦

REGENERATION: NEW BIRTH

What does this mean for the believer today?

The *new birth* is God's way of saving and delivering us today. We have been restored to the position man had available to him before the Fall; regeneration means a change of nature, a new spirit before God. Our spirit man is now alive and new by the power of the Holy Spirit. God wants us to live on the earth as if we were already in heaven, healed, prosperous, and whole in every area of life.

- He has delivered us from the power of darkness and conveyed us into the kingdom of the Son of His love. (Colossians 1:13)

We have the manifestation of God's love and kindness toward us, not because of anything we have done to merit His love but because of what Jesus has done for us. We are being restored and made new by the act of His shed blood and the power of the Holy Spirit's work in our lives. All of God's promises are yes and amen to us. We have the daily hope of the imminent return of our Lord Jesus and are heirs of eternal life!

Regeneration is found in Matthew 19:28 and Titus 3:5. This word means *new birth*. The Greek word so rendered *palingenisia* is used by classical writers concerning the changes produced by the return of spring (www.bible-dictionary.org/Regeneration).

Titus 3:5 symbolizes that change of heart elsewhere spoken of as a passing from death to life; becoming a new creature in Christ Jesus; being born again; a renewal of the mind; a resurrection from the dead; quickened. This change, attributed to the Holy Spirit, originates not with man but with God. The nature of this change lies in implanting a newly formed principle or disposition in the soul, granting spiritual life to those who are already *dead in trespasses and sin.*

As Peter did with Jesus, each believer following the commandments of Jesus will receive the same power from the Holy Spirit without measure so that he (the believer) can do all the works of Christ. Now the works of Jesus Christ are to seek and save the lost, heal, save from Satan, rescue, and deliver men and women from Satan's oppression and set them free spiritually, mentally, and physically. We are brothers and sisters of Christ who know Him and bring honor to our Father in heaven by doing these works. As we have faith to believe in God for this power and authority, God will give it to us in more significant measure.

We are *ambassadors* with royal authority and power in the Messiah's kingdom to rule over the territory God has designated us to rule. We rule over it, or it will rule over us! Our home, each family member, our neighborhoods, our schools, our churches, our local communities, and our places of work. We need to understand our position and responsibility to be trusted with God's mighty miracle and healing restorative working power.

When Jesus had a conversation with Nicodemus, a Sanhedrin member, Jesus conveyed the necessity of *regeneration* and the condition of His death to accomplish a basis for this spiritual transaction. He reiterates this by saying,

- Jesus answered, "Most assuredly, I say to you, unless one is born of water and the Spirit, he cannot enter the kingdom of God. That which is born of the flesh is flesh, and that which is born of the Spirit is spirit." (John 3:5–6)

This scripture was referring to the Holy Spirit being the agent of regeneration. It is a supernatural imparting of eternal life based on Christ's death typified by the serpent Moses lifted in the wilderness.

The Greek word for *be born* in John 3:3 is *genneth anothen*, meaning be begotten from above or having fathered and brought forth from the womb (https://biblehub.com/greek/365.htm).

To be saved, there must be a transformation from God and a renewal in righteousness and true holiness. It is a work of God to transform in us a new creation. Nicodemus misunderstood Jesus in verse 4, asking how a man can enter again his mother's womb; he was thinking only in human terms of the fleshly nature. Millions today make the same mistake in comparing the new birth and the old birth. Water is used in a figurative sense of salvation of the Spirit baptism and the cleansing by the Word of God. Since the Word of God cleanses and regenerates men, being born of water means being born again by the Word. If the Word of God is not read, then there is no cleansing. The Word must be read and followed by taking it into your heart. Liken it to not eating. What will happen to your body if you do not eat for a week or a few months? It is the same with your spirit man; when not fed the Word of God, it will become weak and could die.

Everyone who believes from the heart that Jesus is the Messiah and exercises faith in His atoning blood is born of God, and everyone begotten of God loves both God and man. Loving God and keeping His commandments is proof that we love others, and loving others is proof that we love God.

- Whoever believes that Jesus is the Christ is born of God, and everyone who loves Him who begot also loves him who is begotten of Him. By this, we know that we love the children of God, when we love God and keep His commandments. For this is the love of God, that we keep his commandments. And His commandments are not burdensome. For whatever is born of God overcomes the world. And this is the victory that has overcome the world—our faith. Who is he who overcomes the world, but he who <u>believes </u>that Jesus is the Son of God. (1 John 5:1–5)

Every born-again believer proves their love by loving others and living a Spirit-filled lifestyle. Through His Word, Jesus tells us that in this world, we will have many tribulations and trials. He says that He came to give us peace that passes all understanding. There will be times when we experience discouragement and disappointment. I remember a time when the Lord told me to stop dissing! I was so struck by it that I conducted a word study of many words in the dictionary, beginning with the prefix *dis*. My eyes were opened to God's truth in our beliefs! Adding the prefix *dis* to a word changes the word's meaning. The prefix is negative. The prefix means not or none! With the addition of *dis,* we give the word the opposite meaning. Do you understand that? Satan is a liar! Clearly, I understood that I could not agree with Satan about my belief in disappointment! I asked the Lord for His peace and understanding that He appointed me to do all He has purposed me to do in this season and obey His leading to do it!

Paul writes in Romans that the Jews crucified Jesus because He claimed to be the Son of God; God resurrected Him because He is the Son of God. God says that we need to be obedient to the faith, that this is the test for man in the dispensation of grace. If a man fails to have faith, he is lost.

- Concerning his Son, Jesus Christ our Lord, who was born of the seed of David according to the flesh; and declared to be the Son of God with power according to the Spirit of holiness, by the resurrection from the dead. Through Him, we have received grace and apostleship for obedience to the faith among all nations, for His name: among whom you also are called of Jesus Christ. (Romans 1:3–6)

MOMENT OF REFLECTION

Did you think that God only loves certain people? If so, where did you get that thought?

- And Peter opened his mouth and said: in truth, I perceive that God shows no partiality. But in every nation whoever fears Him and works righteousness is accepted by Him. (Acts 10:34–35)

This scripture shows that all who have sinned can have mercy alike, there being no difference between Jews and Gentiles in God's redemptive plan.

Let's pray.

> Dear Father, Thank You for Your Word. I realize its value and treasure its truth. Your precepts are clearly and purposefully defined to give me direction. Thank You for the wisdom it provides even for the times of our age. Thank You for speaking to me through Your Word. Help me realize its relevance and appreciate how often Your Word addresses the needs of my life. I need Your guidance. I submit myself to You and commit myself to read and study Your Word. May I be faithful as You teach me what I need to learn. In Jesus's name, amen.

Think of those in your family and neighborhood, and unbelievers at work, and pray for them! Ask the Holy Spirit to prepare them to receive Jesus!

10
Chapter

⌇⌇⌇

RESURRECTION POWER
OF JESUS CHRIST

The resurrection power of Jesus Christ is essential. Without it, there will be no salvation, no healings, and no casting out of devils. You need the anointing ability to fulfill Your calling no matter what position you currently have. You will never accomplish what God wants you to do without it. We are all called to minister and serve God; in our everyday lives, we need the Holy Spirit's power to fight devils, sickness, and the power of hell.

So many people want the power of God but fail to understand that it will not come until they first experience His presence. And when His presence comes, the first evidence will be the manifestation of the fruit of the spirit.

- But the fruit of the Spirit is love, joy, peace, longsuffering, kindness, goodness, faithfulness, gentleness, self-control. Against such there is no law. (Galatians 5:22–23)

The ninefold fruit of the spirit is for the character, not for power. In 1 Corinthians 13, the fruit of the spirit is summed up in the word *charity* or divine love. God is love, and all that He is is embodied in His love. No character can be complete without this fruit, and no gift should be exercised without it. The fruit will be evident in regular contact with those around you. And when the fruit is genuinely there, the Lord will anoint you with His Spirit, which is power. Power follows the presence, not the other way around. The presence and the fruit come together. The anointing and the power do too.

When you receive the anointing of the Spirit, the result is the fulfillment of what Jesus said.

- But you shall receive power when the Holy Spirit has come upon you, and you shall be witnesses to Me in Jerusalem, and in all Judea, and Samaria, and to the end of the earth. (Acts 1:8)

In other words, you must have the presence of God in your life first, which will give you the fruit, and this will invite God to dwell within you. Then the anointing will come, which means power. And you will be His witness.

- But the manifestation of the Spirit is given to each one for the profit all. (1 Corinthians 12:7)

The purpose of the manifestation of the Spirit is to build up and help the body of believers. They are the visible healings, miracles, manifest prophecies, tongues, interpretations, and even the wisdom, knowledge, and discernments of various kinds. So they will help everyone who needs them.

Do not covet the gifts of the Spirit to abuse them or to hold them over a brother or sister weaker in the faith. You are lifting yourself up because of the *gift*.

Jesus's death and resurrection on the cross is the power of salvation to us as believers by faith. In Matthew 9, we read that a blind man asked Jesus to heal his eyes. Jesus touched the man, and the man was able to see. Jesus is a merciful Savior, and this man had sufficient faith to see. Your faith strengthens as you read the Bible.

I have given you many scriptures to support this. Your increased faith is dependent on reading the Word of God called the Bible. As believers in this dispensation of grace, we are told to possess the same inherent power to overcome. By believing in Jesus Christ, we can overcome the curse of death because His blood destroyed the devil's works. What does it mean in the life of the believer today? What is sufficient faith?

- My brethren, count it all joy when you fall into various trials, knowing that the testing of your faith produces patience, but let patience have its perfect work, that you may be perfect and complete, lacking nothing. If any of you lacks wisdom, let him ask of God, who gives to all severally and without reproach, and it will be given to him. But let him ask in faith, with no doubting, for he who doubts is like a wave of sea driven and tossed by the wind. For let not that man suppose that he will receive anything from the Lord; he is a double-minded man, unstable in all his ways. (James 1:2–8)

Faith matures and grows to sufficiency when we have exercised the faith of accepted standards of behavior and desperation. Faith like this has nothing to do with external circumstances; it's faith in God's goodness and character that external events can never shake.

It means the same thing to the first-century church: signs, wonders, and miracles should follow those who believe! It means that we are no longer a slave but the child of the true King. It means that now we prosper and are in good health, and we have authority in our family and community.

After everything has been said, the bottom line is that it takes faith in God's ability to be healed.

- So, then faith comes by hearing, and hearing by the word of God. (Romans 10:17)

A person needs to see the Word with their spiritual eyes, hear the Word with their spiritual ears, and understand the Word in their spiritual heart so that their mind is transformed. The result of a transformed mind by the renewing of the Word is healing and wholeness!

- For the hearts of this people have grown dull. Their ears are hard of hearing, and their eyes have closed; lest they should see with their eyes and hear with their ears. Lest they should understand with their hearts, and turn, so that I should heal them. (Matthew 13:15)

God's ways and thoughts are higher than ours. We have His Word to convert us.

- For my thoughts are not your thoughts, nor are your ways My ways, says the Lord. For as the heavens are higher than the earth, so are my ways higher than your ways, and my thoughts than your thoughts. For as the rain comes down, and the snow from heaven and do not return there, but water the earth, and make it bring forth and bud, that it may give seed to the sower, and bread to the eater: so shall my Word be that goes forth out of my mouth: it shall not return unto Me void, but it shall accomplish what I please, and it shall prosper in the thing for which I sent it. (Isaiah 55:8–11)

The Word of God establishes, without a doubt, that it is His will to heal everyone. If we have shown God's will to heal everyone, why isn't everyone healed? And who are the people who still deny God's will to heal today? God knows all the deceitfulness of Satan. Satan has no power to defeat you. He has to deceive you into doubting God's Word.

His purpose is to deceive you into believing religious traditions or man's *vain* philosophy rather than the Word. Religious tradition and worldly thinking will put you in a state of nonresistance. The traditions of men train you to enforce your defeat. Jesus said they make the Word of God of no effect.

The preaching of the Gospel is not complete without healing the sick, casting out demons, and setting captives free. The word *saved* is also translated as *healed*. It is the same *power* that does both. In the same sacrifice that Jesus bore the sin of the world, He bore their sicknesses and diseases. Calvary was a total work. It covered sin, sickness, and mental torment. Jesus came to destroy the results of the devil—all of them. That is what it means in the believer's life today.

Jesus stood up in the synagogue on the Sabbath to read from the prophet Isaiah and said,

- The Spirit of the Lord is upon Me because He has anointed Me to preach the gospel to the poor; he has sent Me to heal the brokenhearted, to proclaim liberty to the captives, and recovery of sight to the blind, to set at liberty those who are oppressed. (Luke 4:18)

In this verse, the Greek word for heal is *iaomia*, which means to heal, cure, restore to bodily health, and when followed by the Greek word *apo*, meaning from, it is a figure of speech of moral diseases. To heal or save from the consequences of sin. The same Greek word, iaomia, is used in the following:

- For the hearts of this people have grown dull, their ears are hard of hearing, and their eyes they have closed; lest they should see with their eyes, and hear with their ears, and should understand with their hearts, and turn so that I should heal them. (Matthew 13:15)

https://biblehub.com/greek/2390.htm
https://biblehub.com/greek/575.htm
The parables in the Gospel of Matthew show Jesus's point that

people do not comprehend what God promises them when they give God their whole heart, mind, and spirit and change their lives. He says the word *should* in Greek means binding is necessary. In other words, when we are converted and believe in God with our whole heart, mind, and body, it is a natural process to be healed in body, soul, and spirit. It's part of the covenant of God!

John 12 reminds us of this point.

- But although He had done so many signs before them, they did not believe in Him, that the word of Isaiah the prophet might be fulfilled which he spoke: "Lord, who has believed our report? And to whom has the arm of the Lord been revealed?" (John 12:37–38)

This quote from Isaiah 53:1 is fulfilled in Jesus's redemptive work on the cross. The ministry of Jesus clearly illustrated and proves that conversion and healing are still for today. Healing is a direct result of conversion. The miracles He performed were done to bring glory to the Father. Because of unbelief, Jesus was rejected and people were not healed. Christians walk in the light!

- Nevertheless, even among the rulers many believed in Him, but because of the Pharisees they did not confess Him, least they should be put out of the synagogue; for they loved the praise of men more than the praise of God. (John 12:42–43)

Paul spoke the same message to the Jews and told them how God's people reacted to Jesus in unbelief. The message remained the same.

- Repent therefore and be converted, that your sins may be blotted out, so that times of refreshing may come from the presence of the Lord. (Acts 3:19)

Our responsibility is to believe in God's promises and provision to us; how can you believe something you have not read or heard? Those who did believe received! *Many* were healed and made whole. In Mark, Jesus tells the blind man that his faith had healed him and made him well. He had immediately received his sight. Here the Greek word for *well/whole* is *sozo*. Because the blind man believed, his eyes were restored and made well. Jesus says that her faith (how she believed) made her physical condition whole again.

The disciple Matthew writes about a woman who walked through a crowd of people while trying to approach Jesus. When she touched the hem of His garment, she believed she would be made whole. She touched His garment when she was close enough, which immediately made her whole. Jesus stopped and said that virtue began to flow from Him when someone touched Him. That word *virtue* means conforming to a standard of right!

- Wherever He entered, into villages, cities or the country, they laid the sick in the marketplaces and begged Him that they might just touch the hem of His garment. And as many as touched Him were made well. (Mark 6:56)

This verse says that *as many as touched him were made well/ whole.* In this verse, the word *whole* is sozo, meaning to save from suffering from diseases or physical injury and restore to health (https://biblehub.com/greek/4982.htm).

It also can mean being saved from danger or destruction.

- And Peter said to him, Aeneas, Jesus the Christ heals you. Arise, and make your bed. (Acts 9:34)

In this verse, Peter demonstrated the same anointing when he healed Aeneas, a man sick with palsy for eight years. This was considered normal healing in the New Testament church. The Greek word for *whole* is iomai, which is to cure, restore bodily health, and could mean that his condition was a result of sin. He believed in the name of Jesus, and immediately he was cured (https://biblehub.com/greek/2390.htm)!

James uses the same context of the word healed, *iomai*.

- Is anyone among you sick? Let him call for the elders of the church, and let them pray over him, anointing him with oil in the name of the Lord. And the prayer of faith will save the sick, and the Lord will raise him up. And if he has committed sins, he will be forgiven. Confess your trespasses to one another and pray for one for another. that you may be healed. (James 5:14–16)

We see this same Greek word for heal, *diasozo*. The same Greek word for *whole*, but translated in these verses as heal, meaning to save through or bring safely through danger, sickness; to preserve.

- And Jesus said to him, "I will come and heal him." (Matthew 8:7)

The centurion believed in the position of authority that Jesus had and faith in Him that if He only spoke the Word of healing, his servant would be healed. What a mighty work God will do when we believe.

- Then He appointed twelve, that they might be with Him and that He might send them out to preach, and to have power to heal sicknesses and to cast out demons. (Mark 3:14–15)

The Greek word for heal here is *therapeuo,* meaning to relieve, heal, cure, to take care of the sick (https://biblehub.com/greek/2323.htm).

Jesus has called and appointed every Gospel minister to do the same works of the ministry of Jesus. The word for heal, therapeuo, is interpreted to mean that as ministers of the Gospel, we are to use our hands just as a physician would minister the healing power of God to cure the sick and heal all diseases. We are to wait upon them as voluntary service. The same word for heal, therapeuo, is used in Matthew 10. Matthew tells us that freely we have received, and freely we give. As ministers of the Gospel, we serve the same way Jesus helped us. The only requirement is to believe!

- And they cast out many demons, and anointed with oil many who were sick, and healed them. (Mark 6:13)

The Greek word for healed is the same therapeuo. It is illustrative in this verse of caring for the sick, serving them. Again, in Luke 9:2 and 10:9, the same Greek word for heal, therapeuo, is used to relieve them of diseases and cure them with the same power (anointing) of Jesus.

- "Lord, have mercy on my son, for he is an epileptic and suffers severely; for he often falls into the fire and often into the water. So, I brought him to Your disciples, but they could not cure him." Then Jesus answered and said, "O, faithless and perverse generation, how long shall I be with you? How long shall I bear with you? Bring him here to Me." And Jesus rebuked the demon, and it came out of him, and the child was cured from that very hour. (Matthew 17:15–18)

After this, the disciples asked Jesus why they could not cast the demon out. He responded that it was due to their unbelief.

The word *cure* is the same Greek word therapeuo, meaning the same thing, to relieve them of the disease and demonic oppression resulting from sin.

There are many other verses of scripture where the Greek words for heal, meaning *whole*, are used to illustrate the power of God to bring about a state of being as saved and made *perfectly whole*. There are many scriptures concerning healing, and I would like to encourage you to go to your concordance and read the scripture given for that word. You will find many resources to identify the word *heal* used in the scripture if you search online.

MOMENT OF REFLECTION

Did God create man to be poor, helpless, sick, and sinful?

The purpose of man's creation is to be prosperous, healthy, successful, happy, wise, and blessed with all the good things he desires. It also includes the cooperation of man to receive the blessings of God. The Creator made all things for the good and pleasure of man. God would not have offered man these things if he were sinful to possess them. No child of God should have to endure the things Christ died to take from him in this life. The promises of God do not require anyone to submit to the devil's work. Demon forces continue to wage war on the saints, trying to persuade them to accept false understandings of God, to assume that sickness, pain, and things contrary to God's will are, in fact, God's will.

Here are some hindrances to answered prayer:

1. Uncertainty in the mind and heart concerning the will of God.
2. Some question if it is God's "time" to bless them.
3. Others question whether it would be best for them.
4. Some question if it is God's will for them.

What to do to *stop* wavering:

1. Study the Bible and become settled about what God promises for all men and women today.
2. God has promises for all our specific human needs.
3. Search for the particular scriptures concerning what you are lacking.
4. God's Word is yes and amen to them who believe.

When you get God's Word on that need, pray in that way. He will answer you. If you do not receive an answer right away, continue to pray until it is answered. The law of faith must be obeyed.

Let's pray.

> Father God, thank You for Your mercy, and it is new every day! I appreciate Your response to my prayer in every way. I live my life for You because You are a faithful God. Your goodness never fails. Your closeness strengthens my faith. The thrill of being transformed into Your glorious body and being able to share a lifetime with You remains strong within me. In Jesus's name, amen.

11
Chapter

❧

LAW OF FAITH

- But without faith, it is impossible to please Him, for he who comes to God must believe that He is, and that He is a rewarder of those who diligently seek Him. (Hebrews 11:6)

According to the Bible, faith is everything. The Bible contains many scripture references about faith, too many to mention here. I would like you to do a New Testament study on faith. Go to a Bible study tool and input *New Testament scripture on faith.* Spend a month meditating on those scriptures and see what God will do!

As you now understand, they promise everyone whatever they believe in (according to God's will) can be obtained. There are no limitations to the *known needs* of this life or the life to come, so do not limit them. You should avoid asking for things that will be about your lustful carnal nature as a word of advice. Ask for your needs in faith, believing you will have a prosperous, healthy life. *There is a way of attaining all of life's necessities.*

Faith is not feeling that prayer is answered. In the limited knowledge of the law of faith, a person seeking to exercise faith is restricted to what they can see, hear, or feel. Sense faith is based on physical evidence or upon the emotions and feelings of the soul. Everyone who takes this road as the basis of faith will sooner or later be deceived. No matter what sense knowledge or feeling knowledge we have, our faith should be based on God's Word.

You will not get an answer to your prayer without faith. If someone refuses to believe, they cannot receive anything from God. It is possible to have faith in God, or it would not be mandatory, as Jesus commanded.

The failure to have faith would mean breaking the law of God and committing sin. In the event they could only realize that it is a sin to be unbelieving, they might be moved to take action against such lawbreaking. Men and women have had trouble believing because they regard unbelief and doubt as natural and cannot be changed. There has been a sense of indifference about it. In an easy situation, there is no problem, but if it becomes a struggle and hard to accept, it is passed off as something beyond our control. The devil uses this to his advantage over people who pray. There is the idea that not all believers have confidence in God, and if one cannot, then it is OK to live in unbelief, to doubt, and to waver at will.

It is common for men and women to assume that if prayer is not answered, it is not God's will to answer. They have abandoned the process of getting an answer, and they are content with being defeated. Because of this, people assume that if their prayers are not answered, it will be OK and that God will not answer the prayer.

When men and women don't receive much, they have little faith. The more they receive, the more faith they have. In the event they waver, they do not get anything. If they only believe in one thing, they only receive one thing. It is not the fault of God if a person gives up in a battle and stops believing in what they asked. They accuse God of being unfaithful and untrue to His Word when it is their fault.

Faith has no relationship with feelings or sense evidence of any kind. Grace and faith in God and His Word are the only grounds for God to answer prayers.

True faith does not rely on the goodness and faithfulness of another person. Faith in God and His Word must come from the heart.

- But let him ask in faith, with no doubting, for he who doubts is like a wave of the sea driven and tossed by the wind. For let not that man suppose that he will receive anything of the Lord, he is a double-minded man, unstable in all his ways. (James 1:6–8)

No person should expect to get anything from God if he refuses to have faith. There is no such thing as the impossibility of having faith, so the fact that one does not have faith is one's own choice and responsibility.

- So, Jesus answered and said to them, "Have faith in God." (Mark 11:22)

I read this scripture above as saying, "Have faith in the *ability* of God to work on your behalf." We cannot do what God can and will do. All the blessings of God come through faith. The law of faith is about believing what God can do. Unless you know what God will do, you cannot believe.

- Jesus said to him, If you can believe, all things <u>are</u> possible to him who believes." (Mark 9:23)

The people of God have been rebuked for lack of faith but never for asking great things from God. God is the one who will answer, and it is His ability, not ours. After prayer, our part is to believe and refuse to doubt.

A few tips to increase your faith:

1. Get "into Christ." Believe everything has changed, including unbelief, and that everything now belongs to God. When you pray, what is the will of God? Paul instructed us, "Pray about everything." They asked Jesus to teach them how to

pray, and Jesus replied that they should pray daily by talking to the Father and asking in His name.

2. Know the Word of God. It is necessary to read and ponder God's Word day and night. It may be hard at first to hear what God has to say about your life and its purpose, but it soon becomes an exciting experience. People rarely consider what God has to say about their requests when they pray. If someone is asked what promise of God is the basis of their faith, they would probably not be able to specify one particular passage.

3. Trust God's Word. It is impossible for God to answer prayers for faith, as they are prayers of unbelief that cannot be answered. You can only have answered prayers if you have the Word as your foundation. God does not instruct us on praying for faith but rather how to feel confident in Him.

4. Put confidence in God and His ability to answer you. Each day, a man or woman and God should have a simple exchange of words. Prayers would be answered without much effort if only they believed.

5. Good preaching versus bad preaching. The miracles of God are described in the scriptures, which are essential for Christians. As we begin to realize what God has done, and will do, to live forever with us, we begin to understand the extent of His involvement. Our faith is undermined when the pastor derides these miracles, calls them fairy tales, or explains their significance in a way that is unclear to us. It is impossible to listen to this kind of preaching and not have questions about something if you hope to have a firm and unwavering faith. Do not allow anyone or any church to slander God or His Word.

6. Exercise your faith to see it grow. Utilize the faith that you have. When faith is used in dealing with all life problems, it will naturally increase, and God will supernaturally ensure that it increases. As a result, you will be filled with the right

kind of faith, demonstrating the proper understanding of human faith. The fall would not have been possible if there was no doubt and unfaith in God and His Word. God intends that man realize He is faithful to His Word and means exactly what He says before answering prayer. To live forever with God, a man must learn faith and absolute confidence in Him sooner or later. The ideal time to learn this is during probation, awaiting the righteous judgment of God.

7. Yield to the Holy Spirit. In addition to being a characteristic of the soul, faith is also a fruit of the Holy Spirit and a gift from God. Through their faith in God and His Word, people who use their faith correctly receive supernatural power from God and become part of the divine nature. The fruit of the spirit will naturally manifest in their lives as they walk and live in the Spirit. When a person believes in union with the divine, everything is possible. Let us all believe in Christ, in the Holy Spirit, in the Word of God, in the atonement, and all the Gospel truths.

MOMENT OF REFLECTION

What must you learn and practice if you want prayers answered? What are your concerns about faith?

Concerning faith in God, there are many things to consider. Take some time to read and meditate on your level of *faith* in trusting that God wants to answer all your prayers.

A father went to Jesus to ask that the devil be cast out of his son.

- Jesus said to him, "If you can believe all things are possible to him who believes." Immediately the father of the child cried out with tears, "Lord, I believe; help my unbelief!" (Mark 9:23–24)

Let's cry out to God today to ask for help with our unbelief. Over time, how much we grow in our belief depends on our willingness to

- let go of trying to control
- submit to God's will
- trust in God's ability

Let's pray.

Lord, we realize that we want to be in control of everything. I confess that I am walking in unbelief when I ask You to help me. Forgive me for my unbelief. Help me believe and receive Your blessings in all areas of my life. By submitting my will to Yours, I trust You can bring about all You have planned and purposed for my life. Thank You, Father. In Jesus's name, amen.

12
Chapter
ᨌᢀᨗ

WALKING WITH GOD

What does it mean to walk with God? How can we do that? According to the most common understanding, the fruit of the spirit is the result of the Holy Spirit working within us. Our relationship with Jesus is filled with the Holy Spirit, and His fruit (God's character) begins to grow in us. Our Lord begins working in us during our conversion, sanctifying and making us more like Jesus (if we allow Him).

Apostle Paul's message is that all who receive the Gospel of the kingdom become citizens of heaven and are freed from the bonds of slavery to the god of this world, Satan. He prays that all believers would be filled with the knowledge of His will in all wisdom and spiritual understanding.

- That you may walk worthy of the Lord, fully pleasing Him, being fruitful in every good work and increasing in the knowledge of God; strengthened with all might, according to His glorious power, for all patience and longsuffering with joy; giving thanks to the Father who has qualified us to be partakers of the inheritance of the saints in the light. He has delivered us from the power of darkness and conveyed us into the kingdom of the Son of His love, in whom we have redemption through His blood, the forgiveness of sins. (Colossians 1:10–14)

In Galatians 5, we read what *the works of the flesh* are versus the *fruits of the spirit.* I ask that you read Galatians 5:16–22 to know what Paul says about *walking in the Spirit.*

What are the good fruits we should strive for to be known by them? *Fruits of the spirit* are *moral standards* that Christians should cultivate in their hearts and minds, according to the apostle Paul.

This verse becomes more personal when we recognize that *fruit* can mean *action, result,* or *deed.* The believer's life will be marked by the fruit of the spirit: love, joy, peace, forgiveness, kindness, goodness, gentleness, and self-control when the Spirit is allowed to work.

In Galatians 5, we also read that the fruit of the flesh is actions, results, or deeds of the carnal, fleshly nature. They are listed as sexual immorality, impurity, sensuality, idolatry, sorcery, enmity, strife, jealousy, fits of anger, rivalries, dissensions, divisions, envy, drunkenness, orgies, and things like these. Paul warns Christians that those who do such things will *not inherit* the kingdom of God.

After repentance and baptism, God gives the Holy Spirit to Christians as one of the greatest gifts. When we do not have the Holy Spirit and are not led by the Holy Spirit, our fleshly works will show and we will not inherit God's kingdom. By God's Spirit guidance, we become *sons and daughters of God* and *heirs of God.*

While it may seem like we're sinking under a sea of stinky, trashy, and rotten circumstances, the Bible instructs us to remain stable and fixed on what God says.

- For he who sows to his flesh will of the flesh reap corruption, but he who sows to the Spirit will of the Spirit reap everlasting life. (Galatians 6:8)

Thus, if we say, "I can't help it," after we sin, we directly *deny* that God gave us self-control along with our new heart. When we operate by the Spirit, not resisting and not merely tolerating sanctification, but joyfully embracing whatever will make us more like Jesus. We then see the results of the fruit of the spirit manifesting in our life. According to Paul, our fallen nature is inherently hostile to God. Unfortunately, we inherited this nature from Adam, and it has not been eliminated since being born again as Christians. God has given us the Holy Spirit, which can keep the flesh from dominating us. God will do His part if we do our part. Our part is yielding to the help of the Holy Spirit.

When I would give a teaching on fruit of the spirit versus the fruit of the flesh, I would often ask the women, "Do you know what is right and what is wrong?" They would look at me as if they didn't understand what I was saying. The humanistic philosophy teaches that whatever feels right is right, regardless of the consequences. They acknowledge their fleshly nature rules over the Spirit of God within them, and they do not want to change.

- And this is the condemnation, that the light has come into the world, and men loved darkness rather than light because their deeds were evil. (John 3:19)
- Then Jesus spoke to them again, saying, "I am the light of the world, he who follows Me shall not walk in darkness but will have the light of life." (John 8:12)

Selfishness, whining, petty jealousies jockeying for power in our workplaces and marriages, the lure of pornography, and the desire for money and possessions often come from the "feelings" of the fleshly nature. Negative, destructive, and addictive actions are the fruits of the flesh. It is a never-ending cycle of gratifying the evil nature; the more it gets, the more it wants, and the sinful nature always wants more. *Right* to the worldly nature directly conflicts with the born-again spiritual nature. When the *fleshly nature* is allowed to *dominate*, it crushes all that is good. In addition to being destructive to the spirit-person, it also inflicts harm and damage on others. It is also physically damaging over the long term. Poor habits endanger physical health from the beginning to the end.

Yet listening to evil (our carnal nature or the devil) separates us from God, making it harder to hear His voice. There is no "life" on that road for eternity or while we are alive on earth.

- "But those things that proceed out of the mouth come from the heart and defile a man. For out of the heart proceed evil thoughts, murders, adulteries, fornications, thefts, false witness, blasphemies. These are the things which defile a man, but to eat with unwashed hands does not defile a man." (Matthew 15:18–20)

Throughout the day, we make choices that affect our lives. Good or bad choices are available to us. It is possible to allow the Spirit of our heavenly Father to lead us. He empowers us to do right. It is clear to Him when to turn and at what speed. Sometimes our choices have a far-reaching impact. Whether a person or a community, we can always influence outcomes.

Isn't it better to let God be the faithful Lord and let us live to please the Father, just like Jesus did? All that matters is that we stay in Him and that He remains in us. As we abide in the Lord and grow in Him, we become more enlightened and continue His plans for us.

When we trust in God, we gain confidence. As we follow the Holy Spirit's guidance, we gain confidence. There will never be smooth sailing on this planet before Christ returns, but when Christ is our Captain, He knows how to take us through rough waters, and He can even calm them.

Let me now share a few other personal times with the Lord. I felt alone and unwelcome at church when facing a very challenging situation. Studying the scripture, I discovered that Jesus communed with God the Father *by the sea*. Taking a walk on the beach, I communicated with my Father, God. I noticed a man holding his little daughter's hand, walking together. My Father spoke to me. "That is you and Me."

From that moment on, I felt so close and secure in Him because I could visualize that moment for comfort. Another time, during a dream, I was swimming in a river with a very strong current pulling me down to drown me. As I asked God for help, he said, "Just float," and with those words from Him, I became calm and remained above the water. I applied that to various circumstances in my life and would *float* through them. I was a swimmer in my younger days and could float and always remained above the water no matter the current. So I was able to understand what He meant. He used my life event to bring me through this tough time in my life.

Every action we take, seen or unseen, is life and death in some way. We can give the Father the honor and glory He deserves by choosing life. Others can benefit from our blessings.

- If you abide in Me, and My words abide in you, you will ask what you desire, and it shall be done for you. By this My Father is glorified, that you bear much fruit; so you will be My disciples. (John 15:7–8)

You can crucify the flesh simply by starving it out. When you starve the flesh while feeding your spirit, the spirit will begin to dominate the flesh. Fasting is all about starving the flesh while feeding the spirit with prayer, Word, submission, humility, and obedience. You are preparing your spirit to tell the flesh no! This applies to food, but the food is a kind of training for the real application. To obtain great spiritual strength, this principle and practice needs to be applied to every aspect of fleshly desires: sexual immoralities, idolatries, distractions, entertainment, emotions, and temperance. Each time we struggle with fleshly lusts, we must adopt a fasting mentality. If your flesh is strong and the spirit is weak, you need to declare a fast of what your flesh wants. Depriving the flesh of power is the only way to make the flesh submit. That means you have to prevent it from getting what it wants. You feed and strengthen your spirit and starve and weaken your flesh by denying it what it wants while giving it what it needs until eventually your flesh dies and you can walk fully in the spirit.

Don't try to fight flesh with flesh. Strengthen your spirit by feeding it the Word of God, worshipping Him, and spending time in His presence. As you consume more of God, the more His Spirit will grow and strengthen within you, and when this happens (in conjunction with intentionally weakening your flesh through depriving it of power), the Spirit will rule in your heart and your life.

I recall a time when I struggled to keep my faith fixed on the things of God. As I prayed, I heard the Lord say, "Draw a line." Considering my concern and what I heard the Lord say, I realized that I had crossed over into the kingdom of darkness. As I saw it, the problem was so significant that it took over the light of God. Truthfully, we can either believe God and His Word or believe a lie from the father of lies. Our faith and ability to receive must be based on the power of God's Word and the Holy Spirit. Our choice is to walk in the light and love of Jesus or cross over to darkness and Satan's lies. We have a choice! My mind was filled with doubt and unbelief. We can trust God to tell us *when* we ask because He is a loving and merciful Father.

I want to share another real-life story of God bringing light out of the darkness with you! Years ago, I volunteered at a local home for unwed mothers and led a weekly Bible study about their identity in Christ. The Lord spoke to me about understanding this principle of "drawing the line and choosing" as I prepared for that class. I was given the title "Salvation: What's in It for Me?" Having studied this already, I believe I knew what he wanted me to teach: being delivered from the kingdom of darkness into His marvelous light and all the benefits of His truth.

A young woman was lying on the couch with her back to the circle at the beginning of the evening. In my mind, I wanted to tell her to get up and get involved or to go to her room. The Holy Spirit very firmly said no!

Rather than speaking to her, I began to pray and teach God's benefits to His children. At the end of the teaching, the young lady was sobbing. She turned around and said that she never knew that! She believed that God would not help her since she was doing drugs when she found out that she was pregnant. In response, I assured her that God would never abandon her, that He wanted to help her. She gave her heart to the Lord that evening, and we prayed that all His benefits would be available to her. She asked for forgiveness for taking drugs and said she would not have taken them if she knew she was pregnant. As a result, she prayed to the Lord to protect and heal her child if any drugs hurt her baby.

Thank God I listened to Him. The following week, I thought I would see this young woman again. There was no sign of her; I asked the girls where she went. One of the other women said an attorney came and told her that a family wanted to adopt her baby. They would pay for her expenses and future needs. Wow! Isn't that just like God our Father! I did not see her for about two years. I was working a part-time job at a local grocery store. Suddenly, I noticed someone waving and saying, "Hey, do you remember me?" She came over to me and told me what had happened after that evening. The child was perfectly healthy and had been adopted by a Christian family. Their goal was to get her involved in seeing her child, and they paid for her to attend Bible college! My heart still gets chills when I think of what God will do for us if we cry out for truth!

We cannot deny it! God is true, His Word is true, Jesus is faithful, and the Holy Spirit is with us!

Has the Holy Spirit convicted you of what you deny about God and the truth of His benefits: Jesus and the Holy Spirit? The title of this book is *We Cannot Deny It*. What are you feeding your spirit and soul: fruit of the spirit or fruit of the flesh? It is your choice. If you are struggling with God and His Word, don't hesitate to contact me, and let's reflect together.

Think about the *fruit of the spirit*. As a chaplain at the work-release program, I suggested to the women who were addicted and attending AA or NA meetings to think about how the fruit of the spirit or the fruit of the flesh was impacting their lives daily. Are you walking in the spiritual fruit, or are you walking in the fruit of the fleshly nature of fear, envy, or unbelief? Learn to "catch" your thoughts and investigate your choice to act on them negatively. The Lord wants to say, "Where is the evidence in what you are thinking?"

FEAR is an acronym: false evidence appearing real.

Write down every false word the enemy is presenting to you. Do a Bible search on the opposite meaning of that word, and see what God says about your situation or fear.

While struggling with great fear, I tried that option and did a word search about the opposite (like the Bible says that perfect love casts out fear). During the early hours of that morning, I had a very real visual dream. A bright light shone down and illuminated my environment as I stood at a crossroads in the dark. I saw a dark figure pointing a gun at me. When I tried to tell that thing to leave, my mouth was covered, and I couldn't speak. Paralyzed by fear, I couldn't move. Finally, I was able to say, "Jesus," and it left me!

MOMENT OF REFLECTION

- Finally, brethren, whatever things are true, whatever things are noble, whatever things are just, whatever things are pure, whatever things are lovely, whatever things are of a good report, if there is any virtue, if there is anything praiseworthy, meditate on these things. The things which you learned and received and heard and saw in me, these do, and the God of peace will be with you. (Philippians 4:8–9)

Capture your thoughts and submit them to the Lordship of Jesus Christ, our Savior and Deliverer! Think about that thought and ask, "Where did that come from?" Let God reveal the truth to you.

It amazes me that God answers so many prayers since men and women generally have such slanderous views of God and His Word. Due to incorrect or no teaching, many Christians suffer needlessly across numerous lines. People suffer from a lack of knowledge and faith, as I did so many years ago, lacking a foundation to stand on. When the answer has not yet come to me, I continue praying and seeking God for the truth. Until He grants me wisdom, I will hold onto Him.

Hold onto God for our country, children, churches, work, and community. We live in a Christian country, so we do not suffer as people in other countries or early believers did. We are free to work, worship God, live a free and wholesome Christian life, get answers to prayers, and live an everyday human life with equal opportunities.

- Then Jesus said to those Jews who believed Him, "If you abide in My word, you are My disciples indeed. You shall know the truth, and the truth shall make you free." (John 8:31–32)

Let's pray.

> Lord, I believe. I thank You for Your truth. Please pour out the richest blessings of Your knowledge and wisdom. Please fill me with Your presence so that I can walk in the light of Your love. I desire to see a greater degree of Your fruit of the Holy Spirit. I want to study Your Word. Please show me what to learn. In Jesus's name, amen.

Thank you for reading this book. I pray that it has helped you to *know why Jesus came to save us.* We were indeed without help. Only Jesus can save us from Satan's evil ways. God bless you!

Printed in the United States
by Baker & Taylor Publisher Services